AF866683

THE CODE OF THE WEST

THE CODE OF THE WEST

A Frontier Guide to MODERN LIVING

CHRIS HUNT

Andrews McMeel
PUBLISHING®

The Code of the West copyright © 2026 by Chris Hunt. All rights reserved. Printed in China. No part of this book may be used or reproduced in any manner whatsoever without written permission, except in the case of reprints in the context of reviews.

The authorised representative in the EEA is Simon and Schuster Netherlands BV, Herculesplein 96 3584 AA Utrecht, Netherlands. (info@simonandschuster.nl)

Andrews McMeel Publishing
a division of Andrews McMeel Universal
1130 Walnut Street, Kansas City, Missouri 64106

www.andrewsmcmeel.com

26 27 28 29 30 SDB 10 9 8 7 6 5 4 3 2 1

ISBN: 979-8-8816-1090-6

Library of Congress Control Number: 2026932816

Editor: Kate Zimmermann
Designer: Brittany Lee
Production Editor: Kayla Overbey
Production Manager: Julie Skalla

FSC www.fsc.org MIX Paper | Supporting responsible forestry FSC® C144853

ATTENTION: SCHOOLS AND BUSINESSES
Andrews McMeel books are available at quantity discounts with bulk purchase for educational, business, or sales promotional use. For information, please email the Andrews McMeel Publishing Special Sales Department: sales@andrewsmcmeel.com.

CONTENTS

THE CODE

Live with courage

Keep your word

Look out for your own

Less is more (save your breath for breathing)

Never corner something meaner than you

Treat everyone with respect and dignity (till they prove otherwise)

It's better to be a has-been than a never-was

Always drink your whiskey with your gun hand (to show your friendly intentions)

Do not practice ingratitude

Ride for the brand

INTRODUCTION

The American frontier wasn't for everyone. Most people didn't go, and for good reason. It was dangerous and relentless. You could lose everything—whether it was to a bad winter, a rattlesnake bite, or any one of a million random commonsense mistakes. The people who stayed behind weren't cowards. They were rational.

People stayed behind because they had families to feed, businesses to run, and communities they'd spent generations building. There was infrastructure that worked for them: courts that resolved disputes, markets that were stable enough to plan around, and social norms that were unambiguous and clear. Leaving meant abandoning all that for a gamble with no guarantee. What kept them where they were was the reasonable calculation that the known world, however constrained, was safer than the unknown one.

Those who went were different. Not better. Just *different*. The kind of people who didn't function well within narrow, fenced-in towns, who itched to see what was over the next ridge. They were the type of people who wanted to go their own way, even if it killed them. So the frontier became their crucible. It didn't ask for a résumé. It cared only if you were willing to put forth the effort. It drew the dreamers and the black sheep, those who could and would operate without external structure, who understood that survival depended on something they carried inside themselves.

What emerged out there wasn't law or governance. It was something else. The people who left had to learn how to cooperate, not because someone made them but because they recognized it was the only way to survive, and so a code of conduct slowly emerged. A code that was dynamic, that could flex and adapt, that held because breaking it had consequences, but it was not the kind of code enforced by courts. It was the kind you carry with you.

We're in a new frontier now, and we're going to have to start building our own structures. It's brutal in a different way from its precursor, through the constant erosion of anything solid to stand on. What's required isn't harder work on the old path; it's the ability to step off it entirely. To blaze our own trail when the maps don't match the terrain. To build a compass when the landmarks keep shifting.

That's what this book is for.

The Code of the West—the project, not just this book—isn't meant to provide all the answers. On the frontier, anyone who tells you they have the map is lying or trying to sell something. What the Code of the West will do is give you a framework for making decisions when there's no clear path. A set of principles you can rely on when the infrastructure fails or betrays you. A code you can carry when everything else is designed to be disposable.

It's not salvation. But it might be enough to keep you moving.

PART 1

The Basics

When I sat down to think about what Code of the West was going to be, it started with something simple: the feeling that something was missing. Not just in me but in the culture at large. The things we used to strive for—purpose, honor, resilience—felt like they were fading.

The world moves fast, and somewhere along the way, we lost touch with what really matters. We stopped valuing the things that build a person's character, and instead, we started valuing the ephemeral—money, fame, the fleeting rush of likes and validation, things that have no real weight. We became spectators in our own lives, watching everything happen around us instead of taking part in it. But deep down, most of us know that we need more than that. We crave purpose. We crave meaning. It's hardwired into us.

That's where the idea for Code of the West was born. Not as a way to reminisce about the past but as a way forward. As a way to reclaim those timeless principles that make a person stronger, that make a person whole.

The Code is more than a set of rules; it's a framework. It's how you navigate life with intention. It's about being an active participant in your own story. By doing that, you're contributing to something bigger.

And that's why this manual exists. It's here to show that there's still a way to live with purpose, with meaning.

There's still a way to take control of who you are and how you show up in the world.

Because *how you do anything is how you do everything.*

THE TENETS

A Modern Expression of Timeless Principles

The Code of the West, as it's known today, was never something etched in stone. It wasn't a formal set of laws or a written rule book, but it functioned as a guide for people living in a time when written laws were often too slow to keep pace with the realities of frontier life. In the early days of the American West, where order was scarce, the Code emerged as a kind of social contract. There was an understanding of what it meant to live with honor, courage, and integrity. It filled the gaps that formal law couldn't reach.

But the truth is, the Code of the West was more than just a product of that time. It was an expression of natural laws, which are the kind of principles that transcend any specific era or place. These weren't just rules for surviving the frontier; they were principles for living a good life, no matter where or when you found yourself.

And that's where this modern version of the Code comes in. What I've sought to do here in this text is take those timeless principles and distill them into ten tenets that are relevant to the world we live in today.

These tenets aren't frozen in the past, but they're also not just flexible guidelines you can ignore when it's convenient.

They're a reminder that no matter how much the world changes, there are certain values that remain constant. Values that shape not just who we are but the kind of society we build together.

The tenets of this Code are my way of articulating those principles for the challenges we face today. They're a guide for navigating life with integrity, courage, and purpose, just like the original Code of the West did for those who came before us. But more than that, they're an invitation to step up and live with intention, to take responsibility for yourself and your community, and to play a part in building something bigger than just personal success.

Because at the end of the day, the Code isn't just about individual rules but a way of living that recognizes the connection between personal integrity and the health of the community around you. It's about the idea that when you live by these principles, you're not just improving your own life; you're contributing to something larger. And that's as true today as it ever was.

APPLYING THE CODE TO MODERN LIFE

A Blueprint for Living

The world looks a lot different today from how it did when the original Code of the West emerged. Technology has shrunk distances, society has become more complex, and the challenges we face are less about survival on the frontier and more about navigating an increasingly connected but often disconnected world. But even though the landscape has changed, the need for a guiding code remains the same—perhaps more now than ever.

At its core, the Code is about how we live in relation to ourselves, to others, and to the larger world. It's about personal responsibility, not just as a buzzword but as a way of life. In an era dominated by social media, where we're constantly connected yet often feel isolated, living with purpose and intention has become more important than ever.

The truth is, none of us were fully prepared for the impact that the internet and social media would have on our lives. For most of human history, communication was a face-to-face act, rooted in physical presence and personal connection. But the digital age came at us fast. We adapted to it without a blueprint, letting the tools shape us instead of intentionally shaping how we use them.

Social media, algorithms, and the 24-7 online world aren't inherently designed to make us worse versions of ourselves, but because we didn't take an active stance early on, many of us fell into patterns of behavior driven by the technology itself. We became reactive, allowing the immediacy of notifications, likes, and comments to dictate how we engaged with the world and each other. Instead of seeing these tools as an opportunity to connect in meaningful ways, we often let them pull us into distraction, comparison, and surface-level interactions.

Just as the original Code of the West was an unwritten social contract—a code of honor and conduct that filled the gaps where formal law couldn't reach—it's time we establish a similar framework for our modern world. The stakes today are just as high. It's no longer about physical survival in a harsh landscape but about our emotional, mental, and societal survival in an era of overwhelming noise and disconnection. The values of the Code weren't just useful for navigating the challenges of the frontier; they're essential now, for helping us course correct and regain a sense of direction and purpose.

This modern version of the Code offers an antidote to that drift. It's a way to reclaim agency in a world where so much feels out of our control. It helps us reframe the way we think about challenges, both online and offline. Instead of seeing obstacles as setbacks, they become opportunities to live out these principles.

A difficult conversation at work becomes a chance to demonstrate courage and integrity.

A personal loss becomes an invitation to build resilience.

And every interaction with others, whether in person or online, becomes a chance to treat people with respect and dignity.

In this way, the Code isn't just about surviving the old frontier but about thriving in the modern one. It's about being mindful of the tools we use, recognizing the power they have over us, and deciding to live with intention in spite of it. It's a blueprint for living in modern life, helping us navigate the complexities of today's world with the same timeless values that helped people thrive in the past.

PERSONAL RESPONSIBILITY

The Code as a Framework for Growth

The Code of the West isn't just a set of ideals meant to be admired from afar. It's a framework for living.

At its core, it demands personal responsibility.

It's not enough to simply know the tenets; you have to live them. The real growth begins when you hold yourself accountable to a higher standard.

In a world that often encourages shortcuts and immediate gratification, personal responsibility has become less common, it would seem. But the Code doesn't leave room for excuses. It challenges you to take ownership of your actions, your decisions, and even your mistakes. When you live by the Code, you're not just following a set of rules; you're shaping your character.

But why does personal responsibility matter beyond just you? Because our lives don't exist in a vacuum.

The choices you make ripple outward, affecting the people around you, the community you're a part of, and, ultimately, society as a whole.

When you live with integrity, you set a standard for others.

You show what's possible when someone holds themselves accountable, and you inspire others to do the same.

Here's where the logic comes into play: A community is only as strong as the individuals within it.

When each person in that community strives to be better, when they commit to being honest, to keeping their word, to facing challenges with courage, it strengthens the entire group. It builds a culture of trust, respect, and cooperation. By contrast, when individuals shy away from personal responsibility, they contribute to the breakdown of that community. Trust erodes, and a lack of accountability leads to division and weakness.

When you take responsibility for your actions, it signals to those around you that they can trust you.

They know you'll follow through and that your word means something. This trust is the foundation of any strong community, whether it's your family, your workplace, or your neighborhood. It creates an environment where people feel safe, where they're willing to rely on each other and work together toward common goals.

Living by the Code isn't just about personal improvement. It's also about communal strength. The stronger you become as an individual, the more you contribute to the strength of those around you. And when everyone embraces this mindset, it fosters a community built on resilience, integrity, and mutual respect.

This idea extends further: When you consistently strive to live by the Code, you're not just bettering your own life; you're contributing to a larger effort to create a society where values like honor, courage, and responsibility are lived out. In this way, living a life of integrity isn't just a personal choice; it's a way to actively shape the world around you.

The Code reminds us that we are all interconnected. Your actions influence the actions of others. Your strength can inspire someone else to find theirs. And as more people commit to living by these principles, the community, whether local or national, becomes stronger. Personal responsibility is the spark that ignites larger change.

MINDFULNESS

The Key to Conscious Living and Connection

Mindfulness is more than just being aware of your own thoughts. We all have a responsibility to understand how our actions, no matter how small, can affect the world around us.

In the Code of the West, this idea of mindful living isn't new. Cowboys didn't just ride with purpose; they *lived* with it.

Every decision was deliberate, guided by an understanding that they were part of something larger, whether it was their community, the land, or even the stories they had a hand in creating.

In today's world, mindfulness has an even broader reach. The world has become connected in ways unimaginable just a few generations ago, and our actions, especially online, have an impact that stretches far beyond our immediate surroundings. Social media and technology have made it easy to act impulsively or without consideration, but living mindfully means bringing the same thoughtfulness to your digital interactions as you would in person.

Every post, every comment, every like says something about who you are and what you value. Practicing mindfulness in this context means recognizing that these small acts create ripples. The Code of the West challenges us to live with integrity and intention, not just on the range but in every aspect of our lives. By being mindful of how we present ourselves and how we engage with others, we can build a community rooted in respect, authenticity, and genuine connection.

Mindfulness isn't about being perfect; it's about being conscious.

It's about making sure that what you put out into the world aligns with your values, whether in your personal life, professional life, or online. When you live with that kind of awareness, you not only improve your own life; you also contribute to a culture that values sincerity and respect. It's the kind of culture that the Code of the West has always been about—and one we need now more than ever.

RESPONSIBILITY
The Weight of the Code

Living by the Code of the West isn't just about personal gain or individual success but about recognizing the responsibility we carry, not only to ourselves but to others. *Responsibility* is woven into the very fabric of the Code. Without it, the principles we aim to live by would lack structure and collapse under their own weight.

When we talk about responsibility, it's easy to think in terms of fulfilling obligations or doing what's expected of us. But the kind of responsibility the Code asks for runs deeper than that. It's about taking ownership of your life, your actions, and the impact you have on the world around you. This includes how you treat others, how you show up in your community, and how you create a better future for those who come after you.

Responsibility doesn't just mean stepping up when things go wrong; it means stepping up when things are going right, too. It's about being proactive and intentional in the way you live, understanding that every choice you make ripples out beyond your own life. The decisions you make today affect the people around you and the environment you'll leave behind.

In today's society, where individualism often leads to self-isolation, it's easy to get caught up in personal success or the pursuit of comfort. But the Code reminds us that we have a role to play and a responsibility to contribute to the well-being of others so to ensure that the next generation inherits something worth preserving. We're not just living for ourselves; we're living as part of a broader community.

Responsibility is often seen as a burden, but within the framework of the Code, it's more of an opportunity. It's a testament to your character and your ability to create positive change. When you live with responsibility, you're actively choosing to make your world better—not just for others but for yourself as well. There's a personal incentive in understanding that a stronger, healthier community makes life better for everyone involved, including you.

This concept of responsibility goes beyond our immediate circles. The more self-aware and intentional we become, the more we see how our actions influence the world at large. Whether it's how we contribute to our workplace, how we engage with social media, or how we participate in our communities, responsibility turns personal growth into meaningful progress.

By embracing responsibility, we're not just lifting up others but ourselves as well. There's an incentive to living this way: a better life, a better community, and a stronger future. That's the heart of the Code.

It's not about altruism; it's about recognizing that in helping others and living responsibly, we're ultimately improving our own lives as well.

PERSONAL RESPONSIBILITY
The Foundation of True Freedom

At the heart of the Code of the West is a simple truth: Freedom and responsibility are two sides of the same coin. True freedom doesn't come from doing whatever you want whenever you want. It comes from the ability to govern yourself, to take ownership of your actions, and to make decisions that not only benefit you but also contribute to the greater good.

Personal responsibility is about more than just fulfilling obligations; it's about understanding that every choice you make has consequences. The cowboy knew that when he made a promise, his word was his bond. If he failed to deliver, there were no excuses, only the reality of his choices and the impact they had on others.

In today's world, personal responsibility is no less important. We live in a time where it's easy to shift blame, to point fingers, and to avoid accountability. But the truth is, no one else is coming to fix your problems. No one else can live your life for you. The power to change your circumstances lies in your hands. And that power comes from accepting responsibility for everything within your control.

When you embrace personal responsibility, you reclaim your agency.

You stop being a passive participant in your own life and start steering the ship. This is where true freedom lives. Not in the absence of rules or constraints but in the knowledge that you are in control of your own destiny. When you choose to act with responsibility, you shape the world around you rather than being shaped by it.

Responsibility is also what grounds you in your community. When you show up for yourself, you're better able to show up for others. You become someone people can rely on, someone who contributes to the fabric of a stronger, more resilient society. And in that contribution, you find meaning and purpose that stretch far beyond personal success.

True personal responsibility is not a burden but an opportunity.

It's the chance to create a life that reflects your values, to stand for something, and to live with integrity in every aspect of your existence. When you own your choices, you own your future.

PERSONAL RESPONSIBILITY
The Key to Living with Purpose

Personal responsibility is about owning your life in every sense. Your choices, your actions, and your mindset belong to you and you alone. It's not about setting an impossible standard for yourself but about recognizing that no one is coming to do the work for you. If you want to live with purpose, you need to start by owning your responsibilities. We must recognize that personal responsibility isn't just a burden but an opportunity. An opportunity to shape your life the way you want it to be.

Here's where it all connects: The more you cultivate personal responsibility, the more you tap into your sense of purpose and identity. Purpose isn't something that happens to you; it's something you create by actively engaging with your life. And the more responsibility you take, the more power you gain to direct your own course.

So what does this look like in action?

Here's where the manual comes in. Throughout the following sections, we'll explore practices and mindsets that are key to building this kind of life. From taking ownership of your health to developing resilience, the path to becoming someone who lives with integrity and strength requires commitment on multiple fronts.

It's not just about being capable for the sake of it. This manual will show you that when you invest in yourself, your mental and physical health, and your skills, you become more self-directed. With more capability comes more control, and with more control comes confidence. And that confidence ripples out, influencing not only your life but the lives of those around you.

We'll walk through everything from mindset shifts to hands-on skills that will strengthen your resilience and help you adapt in the face of challenges. Resilience is about more than bouncing back. It's also about knowing how to pivot when life throws you a curveball. And just like personal responsibility, resilience is a skill you build, not something you're born with.

IDENTITY AND PURPOSE
A Holistic Approach

Your sense of identity comes from knowing who you are and where you're headed, but it's also informed by the choices you make each day. Especially by how you handle responsibility and adversity. The more knowledge and tools you gain, the more capable you become, and the more defined your sense of identity grows. Living with purpose is a by-product of this kind of deep self-awareness and intention. You don't just stumble into a purposeful life; you build it.

This manual isn't just a collection of ideas. It's a road map for taking control of your life. Purpose, identity, and resilience don't accidentally show up fully formed one day just because you want them to. It's only after you decide to start owning your responsibilities that you'll find everything else begins to fall into place. And in doing so, you're not just making your own life better; you're contributing to the strength of your community and, ultimately, your country.

BRINGING IT ALL TOGETHER

Throughout this manual, we'll further explore the foundations of the Code of the West, how its tenets and timeless principles translate to our modern lives. This isn't just a set of abstract ideas or moral guidelines; it's a framework designed to empower you. Whether it's through building resilience, living with purpose, or taking responsibility for yourself and your community, the Code offers a way to approach life that brings out the best in you—and in those around you.

We've talked about the importance of personal responsibility, of recognizing that while you may not be able to control everything that happens in life, you have full control over how you respond. We've discussed how self-awareness, grit, and adaptability are not just traits to be admired but tools to be actively sharpened and used in your everyday life. And we've acknowledged the larger context: that the more we each embrace these principles, the stronger and more cohesive our communities, *and our nation,* will become.

The key here is action. This manual is only as useful as what you do with it. The ideas laid out are starting points, but their true power is in application.

It's about showing up every day, making intentional

choices, and building habits that align with the Code. Small actions add up over time.

Every decision, every interaction, every bit of effort you put in moves you closer to living in alignment with these values and, in turn, contributes to a society built on integrity, honor, and resilience.

The challenges ahead of us may seem daunting, but that's exactly why this Code matters now more than ever. It offers a way forward, one that's rooted in timeless principles but adaptable to the unique circumstances of our time. And while the path won't always be easy, it will be worth it. Because in the end, how we choose to live, both individually and as a community and, in turn, a nation, will determine the future we build together.

The time to act is now.

Let this manual be a guide, but let your actions be the proof of your commitment to living with courage, purpose, and responsibility. The world needs people who are willing to step up, lead by example, and embody the principles of the Code of the West. The question now is: Are you ready to take that step?

PART 2

Purpose

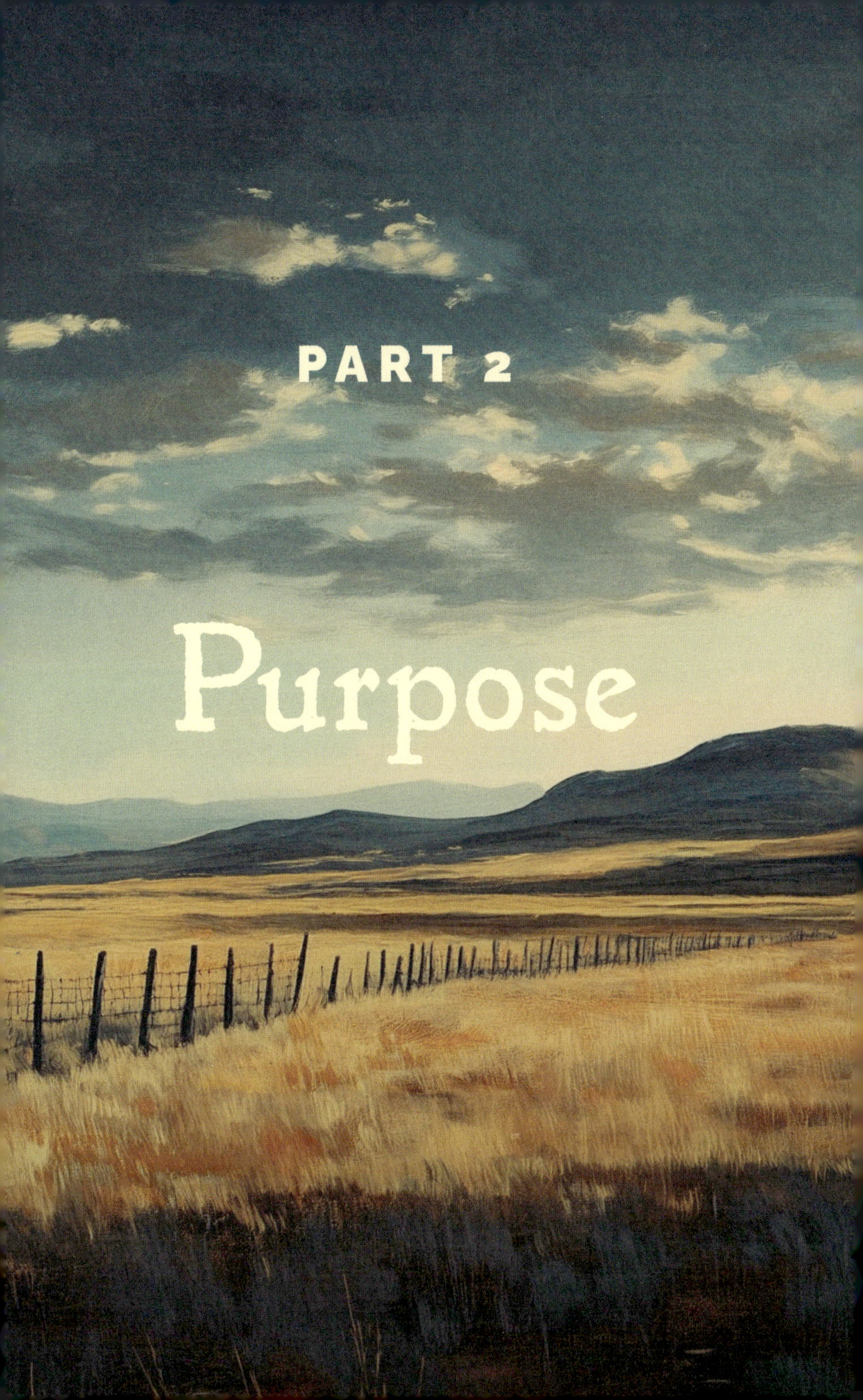

In the heart of every person is a desire to find meaning. Some people search for it in their work, others in their relationships, and some in the small, everyday moments that might seem insignificant but ultimately make up the fabric of a life well lived. But purpose isn't something that's handed to you. It's something you craft, something you build through your actions, your values, and your choices.

The search for purpose can feel daunting in a world that's constantly pulling you in different directions. It can seem like the world is offering endless distractions, convincing you that fulfillment lies just beyond the next click or the next purchase. But true purpose isn't something you stumble upon—it's forged.

It's shaped by the work you do, the values you hold, and the intention you bring to your life every single day.

In this section, we'll look at how purpose shows up in your life. Not as some grand, far-off ideal but as something grounded in the everyday. You'll learn how to approach your work, your relationships, and your commitments with intention, understanding that purpose is a process, not a destination. It's in the way you carry out the smallest tasks, because how you do anything is how you do everything.

This manual isn't about *finding* a purpose; it's about crafting one. And in the process, you'll discover that purpose, once built, gives you something solid to stand on. It gives you the direction to navigate the challenges of life, knowing that everything you do is tied to something greater.

OWNERSHIP

Taking Responsibility for Your Path

At the heart of purpose lies ownership. It's about recognizing that your life, your actions, and your outcomes are your responsibility. This doesn't mean blaming yourself for every setback; you will always be contending with forces outside of your control.

What it means is accepting that you have the power to influence your situation. Owning your path requires you to stop waiting for someone else to come along and fix things. It means stepping up and taking control of the choices that shape your life.

Take, for example, someone who feels stuck in their job.

It's easy to blame the company, the boss, or even the economy. But ownership means looking at the situation and asking, "What can I do to change this?" Maybe it's developing new skills, seeking out opportunities elsewhere, or finding ways to improve your current role. The key is to focus on what's within your control, which, to put it simply, is the intersection of your effort, your mindset, and your decisions.

Owning your path also means being honest with yourself about where you're succeeding and where you need to improve. It's one thing to want a better life, but it's another to admit where you're falling short and take action to fix it. When you own your path, you stop making excuses and start finding solutions.

THE POWER OF ACCOUNTABILITY

Ownership and accountability go hand in hand. It's not enough to take responsibility in theory. You have to follow through in practice. Holding yourself accountable means setting clear standards for your actions and making sure you meet them. For example, if you decide to commit to working out three days a week, ownership is sticking to that plan, even when it's inconvenient or you're tired. Accountability builds trust in yourself, as well as the confidence to know that you will show up for yourself when you say you will.

Another good example of ownership is in personal finances. Many people feel overwhelmed by debt or lack of savings. It's easy to avoid the issue or blame outside circumstances. But taking ownership means sitting down, understanding your situation, and developing a plan to address it. It might not be an overnight fix, but the act of taking responsibility for your financial future sets you on a course for long-term success.

BECOMING THE AUTHOR OF YOUR OWN STORY

In the end, purpose isn't just about what you do; it's about who you become. When you take ownership of your life, you become the author of your own story. It's easy to drift when you let external forces steer you, but when you take the reins, you get to decide where you're headed. Ownership is about being proactive and taking the wheel to guide your life where you want it to go. The more you practice ownership, the more you realize that the life you build is in your hands.

IDENTITY, VALUES, AND THE GREATER GOOD

Your sense of purpose is deeply tied to your identity. "Identity" is the overall person you see yourself as. That can include a lot, but perhaps most important are your values, which are the principles that guide your decisions and actions. Purpose and identity act as the foundation for the kind of life you want to live, and the goals you set should naturally flow from them.

But purpose is about more than just personal fulfillment. When you show up as a capable, responsible individual, you're not only improving your own life; you're contributing to the strength of your community and, ultimately, your country.

The more capable and grounded people we have in America, the stronger and more resilient we all become. A nation is built on individuals who strive to be the best versions of themselves, people who live with courage, integrity, and a commitment to something greater.

Your identity is more than just a label or a role you play. It's a combination of your experiences, the things you care about, and how you want to be seen in the world. The more deeply you understand who you are, the clearer your sense of purpose becomes.

But identity isn't fixed. It's something that evolves over time. As you go through life, face challenges, and pursue goals, your sense of self will change. That's why reflecting on your identity at different points is key to staying grounded in your purpose. The person you are today might not be the same person you were five years ago, and that's okay.

What matters is making sure your goals still reflect who you are now.

And as your identity grows, so does your capacity to contribute to the larger fabric of society. When you commit to living with purpose, you're playing a part in shaping not just your own future but the future of your community and your country.

Values are the principles that define what's most important to you. They guide how you make decisions and interact with the world. When your values are clear, they act like a compass, helping you navigate both everyday choices and major life decisions.

Ask yourself: What do I stand for? What do I believe in? What matters most to me?

Once you have those answers, you can start aligning your actions with those values. Whether it's integrity, courage, loyalty, or responsibility, when you live in a way that reflects those values, you naturally build purpose into your life.

Living according to your values isn't just a personal endeavor; it's a way of strengthening the culture and community you're a part of. When

more people live with integrity and purpose, the collective strength of our country grows. America is only as strong as the people who make it up, and every action you take toward bettering yourself adds to the greater good.

GOAL SETTING

Setting goals is one of the most tangible ways to build purpose. It's how you move from simply existing to actively shaping the direction of your life.

But goal setting isn't just about creating a list of tasks or ambitions. It's about aligning your actions with the bigger picture of who you want to be and what you stand for.

The key to effective goal setting is understanding that purpose is built over time. It's not found in a single achievement but in the steady process of moving toward something meaningful. Your goals, then, should be a reflection of what matters most to you, whether that's in your work, your personal life, or your relationships.

Here's how to set goals with purpose in mind.

1. **START WITH YOUR VALUES:** What do you believe in? What do you care about? When your goals are aligned with your core values, they naturally have more weight and meaning.

2. **BREAK IT DOWN:** Big goals can seem overwhelming, but breaking them into smaller, actionable steps makes them manageable. Remember: Purpose is built in the small, everyday tasks that eventually lead to something bigger.

3. **STAY FLEXIBLE BUT COMMITTED:** Life will throw

curveballs, and your path might not always be clear. But if your goals are tied to something you deeply believe in, it'll be easier to stay the course, even when the road gets tough.

4. MEASURE YOUR GOALS: One of the hardest lessons to learn when working toward a dream is how to measure your progress. It's easy to get caught up in lofty goals—like earning accolades or reaching abstract milestones—but the truth is, success needs a framework. If you can't measure it, how do you know whether you're making progress?

This is where the idea of putting a number to your goals comes in. Whether you're trying to build a career, improve your financial situation, or create something from scratch, you need a tangible benchmark. And sometimes that benchmark is financial. While it may feel strange to attach a dollar amount to your goals, particularly if you're in a creative field, doing so can help ground your purpose in reality.

For example, when I was chasing the goal of becoming a comic book artist, I originally thought success meant publishing books or winning awards. But the truth was that those achievements didn't create the security or sense of fulfillment I was looking for. It wasn't until I set a clear financial goal of earning $100,000 in a year that I was able to create a measurable path to success. I didn't hit it the first year, but it pushed me further than I'd ever gone. And when I finally did, it wasn't just about the money. It was about knowing that I had achieved something I could measure.

You have to be able to measure your goals if you want to reach them. There's nothing wrong with attaching numbers to your goals, especially when it gives you a clear way to track your progress. In fact, it's often the most reliable way to ensure that you're on the right track.

5. REVIEW AND REFLECT: Check in with yourself regularly. Are your goals still aligned with your purpose? Are they bringing you closer to the life you want to live, or do they need adjusting? Purpose evolves, and so should your goals.

Remember that purpose isn't a destination—it's a journey. The act of setting goals and working toward them is what helps you build purpose in your life, step by step.

THE POWER OF COMMITMENT

Staying the Course

Knowing your purpose is one thing, but living it out day after day is another. It's easy to have big ideas and set lofty goals, but the real test of purpose comes in your ability to stick with it when the road gets tough.

That's where commitment comes in. Commitment keeps you anchored when life throws obstacles in your way, and it's the difference between giving up and pushing forward.

Purpose isn't glamorous. In fact, most of the time, it's a grind.

The daily pursuit of purpose involves a lot of unseen work: sacrifices, hard choices, and moments when it would be easier to quit than keep going. But that's exactly when commitment becomes crucial. Purpose without commitment is just an idea, a dream without roots. But when you back up your purpose with consistent action, you turn it into something real.

A lot of people think commitment means tackling the biggest obstacles head-on and charging through adversity without blinking. In reality, commitment is built through the small wins, the daily habits and choices that bring you closer to your goals. It's about showing up every day, even when it feels like progress is slow. Over time, those small actions compound, and before you know it, you'll find that you're farther down the path than you ever thought possible.

The moment you commit to living with purpose, resistance shows up. Sometimes that resistance comes from within, like self-doubt, fear of failure, or even fatigue. Other times, it'll come from the outside in the form of unexpected challenges, setbacks, or people who don't believe in your vision. No matter the source, resistance is inevitable, so learning how to respond to it is key. Every time you push through resistance, you're building resilience and reaffirming your commitment to your purpose.

The truth is, commitment to purpose is less about intensity and more about longevity. Anyone can sprint for a few days or weeks, but the people who achieve something meaningful are the ones who stick with it for the long haul. Staying the course means accepting that there will be days when you don't feel like doing the work but you do it anyway because you know it's part of the larger picture.

BUILDING A LEGACY THROUGH PURPOSE

Your purpose isn't just about what you accomplish during your lifetime but the impact you leave behind. Whether you're aware of it or not, the actions you take, the values you hold, and the example you set will create a legacy that lives beyond you. The question is: What kind of legacy do you want to leave?

Living with purpose means being intentional about the kind of world you want to shape and how you contribute to it. It's about making decisions that align not just with short-term goals but with long-term values and principles. Your purpose is the bridge between your day-to-day actions and the lasting mark you leave on those around you.

The Long Game: Thinking Beyond Today

When you focus on purpose, you're playing the long game. It's easy to get caught up in immediate concerns, whether that's chasing career success, acquiring material wealth, or seeking short-term wins. But the true power of purpose lies in how it extends beyond the present. Living with purpose means thinking about how your actions today will ripple out into the future, impacting not just your life but the lives of others.

Building a legacy requires patience, persistence, and a vision that stretches beyond the here and now. It's about doing the hard work, even when it doesn't pay off immediately, because you know that what you're building is worth it.

Living as an Example

Legacy isn't just about material achievements. It's about the example you set for others in your life, like your family, friends, and community.

It's the principles you live by and the lessons you pass on, whether directly or through the life you lead. Sometimes, the most profound impact you leave behind isn't in the tangible things you accomplish but in the inspiration you give others to live with integrity and courage.

In a world where so much is fleeting, your legacy can be a steady anchor and a testament to what you stood for and the values that mattered most to you.

Purpose in Action

Building a legacy is not some grand, abstract idea. It's created in the daily choices you make. How you treat others, the work you put in, and the challenges you face are the moments that accumulate to define your legacy. Purpose, then, isn't something you stumble upon. It's something you craft, day by day, with intention.

By focusing on purpose, you're shaping the kind of person you want to be remembered as while also contributing to the larger story of your community, your country, and the people who will come after you.

PURPOSE

Bringing It All Together

Purpose isn't something you find; it's something you craft over time. It's not about waiting for a lightning bolt of inspiration to hit but about building something step by step through your choices, actions, and intentions. By exploring what drives you and understanding your values, you start forging a path that's uniquely yours.

First, consistency becomes the foundation. It's the daily, sometimes mundane, commitment to show up even when the excitement fades. With consistency, you start building habits that become second nature, creating a steady rhythm that keeps you moving forward.

Then comes adaptability—the recognition that life will never go exactly as planned. We can't control every twist and turn, but we can choose how to respond. Like a cowboy facing down a storm, your ability to shift, adjust, and keep moving is crucial. The world throws punches, and adaptability ensures that you can stay standing. But none of this sticks without ownership. Taking responsibility for your path means recognizing that, in the end, it's on you. No one else is going to create the life you want. Ownership means having the courage to face yourself honestly, hold yourself accountable, and make the tough decisions that drive your future.

Finally, commitment is what holds it all together. The long game requires both dedication and persistence. Purpose isn't a sprint. It's a lifelong journey, and the strength of your commitment will determine how far you go. The more you invest in your purpose, the deeper the roots grow, anchoring you through the storms of life.

In this section, we've laid out the building blocks of purpose: consistency, adaptability, ownership, and commitment. Each one reinforces the other, creating a structure you can rely on. You don't have to have everything figured out today. What matters is that you're willing to show up and keep building.

Purpose isn't an end goal. It's the way you live your life.

PART 3

Resilience

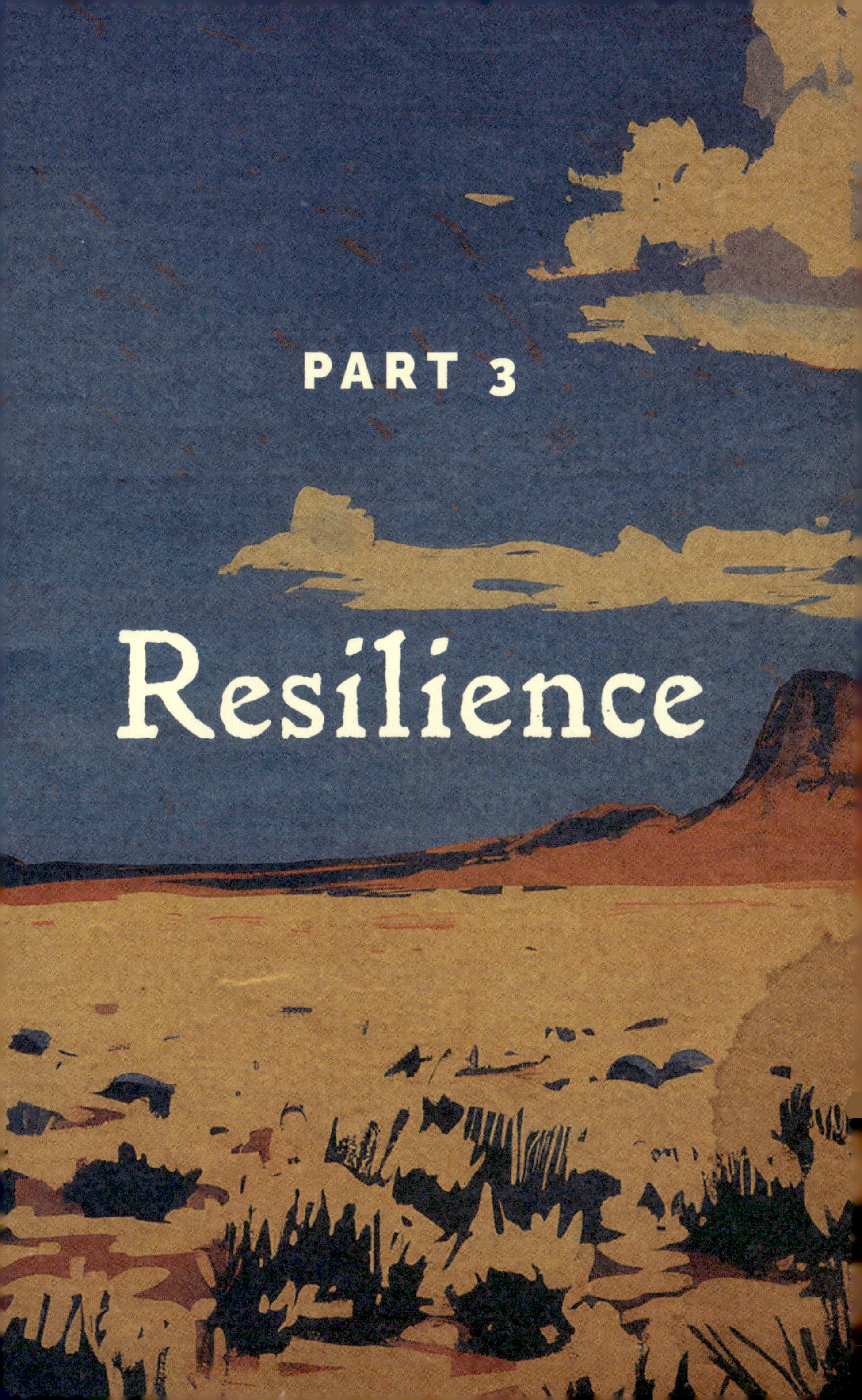

In the previous section, we laid the groundwork with the concept of purpose. Purpose gives us a direction, a reason to show up, to strive, and to push ourselves toward something bigger than ourselves. But as you move toward your goals, as you walk the path you've chosen, challenges are inevitable. This is where resilience comes into play.

Resilience is not about avoiding hardship or difficulty. It's about confronting them head-on, learning how to adapt and recover. Where purpose provides the "why," resilience provides the "how." It's the ability to keep going even when the journey gets tough, even when setbacks occur.

In this section, we'll explore what it means to get back on the horse after being thrown off, to face the storms of life with grit and resolve, and to come out the other side not just as the same person but as a stronger, wiser version of yourself. Resilience is about growth through adversity, and it's deeply tied to the values we hold and the sense of responsibility we carry for ourselves and those around us.

As you move forward, you'll see that resilience is more than just bouncing back. Getting back on the horse, refocusing, and continuing the ride are all parts of living by the Code of the West.

FACING ADVERSITY

Adversity is a fact of life. Whether it's losing a job, suffering a personal setback, or navigating through the unpredictability of the world, hardship is something every person encounters. It's not a matter of whether adversity will come knocking but when. How we choose to respond to these challenges, however, defines who we are and how we grow.

In the Code of the West, there's a simple but powerful truth: "A cowboy isn't measured by how he rides when things are easy but how he rides through the storm." It's easy to stay on course when the sky is clear and the path is smooth, but when adversity hits and the storm rolls in, you find out what you're really made of. That's when resilience comes into play.

The first step to building resilience is accepting that challenges are unavoidable. There's no point in hoping that life will be free of hardship. What matters is how you face the storm. Do you run from it, or do you ride into it? The old cowboy saying goes: "When you get bucked off, you've got to get back on the horse." And it's not just about getting back up but how you get back up *stronger.*

Adversity, in its purest form, is life's way of testing your resolve. It sharpens your instincts, strengthens your character, and teaches you the lessons that only hardship can offer. Those who face adversity head-on not only build their resilience but also gain the respect of others and, most important, respect for themselves.

The most resilient among us are not the ones who avoid challenges but the ones who learn to ride through them. They know that every setback is an opportunity to grow and every storm is a chance to prove their strength. This mindset is the backbone of resilience and the key to thriving, not just surviving.

GRIT

The Long Haul

Grit is more than just surviving a single storm; it's about having the determination to keep going, day after day, long after the initial excitement or motivation has faded. In the Code of the West, grit is seen as one of the highest virtues—not because it's flashy but because it's necessary. A man doesn't earn respect for doing something once. He earns respect for doing it again and again, no matter how tough the road gets.

Grit is what separates those who give up from those who see things through to the end. It's easy to be excited when a journey begins, but as the path gets harder, when the days stretch on, it's the ability to keep putting one foot in front of the other that defines success. Whether you're working toward a long-term goal, facing down a tough personal challenge, or simply trying to navigate through life's ups and downs, grit is what keeps you moving forward.

It's not the speed that matters but the direction and persistence. You might not be the fastest or the strongest, but if you keep showing up, keep putting in the work, and keep pushing through when others have quit, you'll reach the finish line. And that's where the reward lies. Not in the grand gestures but in the daily grind, the small but steady efforts that compound over time.

Grit also builds character. It's not just about reaching the destination but about who you become along the way. With every day that you stick to it, you become more resilient, more capable, and more prepared for whatever comes next. And in a world that's often focused on instant gratification, there's a certain quiet power in the ability to endure. It shows a depth of character that's hard to ignore, and it earns a respect that's impossible to fake.

In the end, grit isn't just about surviving. It's about thriving, even when the road is tough. It's about the long game, the understanding that true success isn't built overnight but over weeks, months, and years of steady effort. At its heart, that's what the Code of the West is all about: showing up, day after day, with the strength to keep going, no matter how long the journey takes.

MENTAL TOUGHNESS

Strength in Vulnerability

In the previous section, we talked about grit, which is the ability to stick with something even when it's hard. Mental toughness builds on that grit, but it's more than just getting through tough times. It's about how you choose to face those challenges and whether you truly grow from them or just perform endurance for the sake of appearances.

There's a difference between showing up and doing the work and just showing that you're working. The difference is subtle but important. Activity doesn't always equal achievement. We live in a world where it's easy to put on a show, to make sure everyone sees how hard you're working or how much you're struggling. But real mental toughness isn't performative. It's quiet. It's about doing what needs to be done, whether or not anyone is watching. The cowboy rides through the storm not because he's looking for admiration but because he knows that's what the journey requires.

And here's where the distinction really matters: There's a huge difference between complaining and asking for help. Complaining is about broadcasting your discomfort for sympathy or attention. Asking for help, on the other hand, takes courage. It's recognizing that no one can carry the full weight of life alone and that there's strength in leaning on others when you need to.

A cowboy might ride solo most of the time, but even the toughest riders know when it's time to reach out to a partner. It takes more strength to admit you need help than to pretend you've got it all handled. Mental toughness isn't about being invincible; it's about knowing when to push through and when to rely on the people around you.

True mental toughness is about staying the course with integrity, whether the world sees it or not. It's not about activity for the sake of activity. It's about meaningful progress and knowing that sometimes real strength is found not in silence but in the courage to speak up and seek support.

ADAPTABILITY

Rolling with the Punches

There's an old saying: "Everybody has a plan until they get punched in the nose." It's a simple way of saying that no matter how much you prepare, life tends to throw unexpected challenges across your path. When things go off track, adaptability is what separates people who get stuck from those who find new ways to keep moving forward. It's the ability to change your approach without losing sight of your greater purpose.

Adaptability doesn't mean that you abandon your goals. It just means finding new routes to get there. Think of it like crossing a river. If the bridge is washed out, it's not about turning around and going home; it's about finding another way across. The people who succeed aren't the ones who stick stubbornly to a broken path but those who are willing to pivot without sacrificing their destination. In life, jobs change, circumstances shift, relationships evolve, and even your physical health can throw curveballs. Flexibility is about recognizing when it's time to take a different approach, whether that's learning a new skill or accepting that a certain plan just isn't going to work. When you stay flexible and adaptable, you're not tied to a singular vision of how success should look. Instead, you're anchored by the deeper values that give your life meaning. That's why flexibility is so important. It allows you to adjust your methods while holding on to what matters most.

There's a big difference between your plan and your purpose. Plans are just road maps, subject to change with the terrain, but purpose is what keeps you headed in the right direction, no matter what detours you encounter. You can prepare and strategize and have everything in place, but sometimes life doesn't care about your plan. That's when adaptability becomes your greatest asset. The key to maintaining your purpose is being willing to change tactics when necessary.

Picture someone who's lost a job or missed out on an opportunity. It's easy to feel like the rug has been pulled out from under you.

But if you see your career as a vehicle for your larger purpose, whether that's providing for your family, serving your community, or achieving personal goals, then losing one job doesn't mean you've lost everything. It just means it's time to find another vehicle. Maybe it's not the one you expected, but if you stay adaptable, you'll find another way to keep moving forward.

People often think of resilience as bouncing back from adversity, but it's more than that. It's about taking the hits and using them to fuel your growth. Resilience is what turns setbacks into stepping stones. Each time you adapt, each time you find a way through the chaos, you become stronger and more equipped to handle whatever comes next.

When life delivers that proverbial punch to the nose, adaptability is the thing that keeps you on your feet. It's not about whether you get knocked down (everyone does at some point). It's about how quickly you can reassess and get back up. Those who thrive don't wait for things to go back to normal. They adjust, they recalibrate, and they push forward. Over time, this kind of resilience becomes second nature. It's what allows you to keep growing even when the world around you is changing faster than you can keep up.

There's a strange kind of freedom that comes with being adaptable. When you let go of rigid expectations and embrace the idea that change is inevitable, you stop fearing the unknown. Instead, you start seeing it as an opportunity. The more you practice adaptability, the less you'll be shaken by surprises. You'll learn to meet each challenge head-on, knowing that you have the flexibility and the purpose to navigate through it.

Think of it like our cowboy who rides into the storm. He knows he can't control the weather, but he can control how he rides through it. The storm might slow him down, change his course, or force him to find shelter, but he's not going to let it stop him. He knows where he's headed, and he trusts himself to get there, no matter how rough the journey becomes.

Your purpose isn't about sticking to a script; it's about staying true to what drives you, no matter what happens. Adaptability allows you to ride out the storms and keep pushing forward, even when the plan falls apart. It's the trait that keeps your purpose alive, even in the most uncertain times. Every time you adapt, you're proving that your purpose isn't just a fleeting idea but something deeply rooted in who you are.

In the end, adaptability is what keeps you moving forward when the world around you feels unstable. It's not about perfection, and it's certainly not about always getting things right. It's about being willing to change when change is needed, without losing sight of who you are and what you stand for.

SUPPORT NETWORK

The Backbone of Resilience

No one is meant to go through life alone. While grit and mental toughness are essential, having a solid support network is equally important. The people we surround ourselves with—our family, friends, mentors, and colleagues—can either help us stand stronger or unknowingly hold us back. Resilience isn't just about your own strength; it's also about knowing when to lean on others.

In the Code of the West, cowboys ride solo at times, but even the most seasoned riders know the importance of a good partner or crew. A strong support network doesn't just offer help in hard times; it provides perspective, guidance, and encouragement when you need it most. It's about surrounding yourself with people who push you forward, challenge you to grow, and remind you of your values when life gets rough.

But not every support network is healthy. A negative network might look like a group of people who validate complacency, fuel negativity, or even undermine your resilience by keeping you stuck in bad habits or thought patterns. These are the friends who discourage you from trying new things, keep you in your comfort zone, or criticize your efforts without offering solutions. Over time, this kind of network erodes your resilience and makes it harder to stand tall when challenges arise.

A strong support network, on the other hand, calls you to your best self. They don't shy away from telling you hard truths, but they do so with the intention of helping you grow. They remind you of your strengths when you've forgotten them, and they're there to help you get back on the horse when you've been bucked off.

Choose your circle wisely. Your resilience depends not only on how strong you are but also on the strength of the people who stand beside you. Just as a cowboy needs a good horse and reliable companions for the journey, you need people who will ride alongside you, helping you stay the course when the going gets tough.

RESILIENCE IN ACTION

Bringing It All Together

Resilience isn't just a concept you can simply read about but rather something you live, day in and day out. Something you must *embody*. Whether you realize it or not, every time you face a challenge and keep moving forward, you're practicing resilience. But what does that look like in real-world terms?

Imagine a cowboy out on the range. He's prepared for the ride ahead, but the path he planned is washed out, and the weather is making it impossible to see more than a few feet ahead. This cowboy has two choices: Turn back and wait for the storm to pass, or find another way forward.

First, his grit kicks in. He knows he's been through storms before, and he's still standing. Grit reminds him that he's got what it takes to push forward. Next, his mental toughness guides his decision-making. Instead of just enduring the storm, he's looking for opportunities to find shelter, to chart a new course, or to simply ride smarter. He's not pretending to be invincible; he knows when to hunker down and when to ask for help.

Speaking of help, maybe he's not alone out there. His support network could be a fellow rider or someone back at the ranch on the other end of a radio. The strength in asking for assistance isn't weakness but wisdom. And finally, adaptability gets him through the storm. When one route doesn't work, he tries another. When the terrain changes, he adjusts his approach. The storm won't stop him. It'll just make him a better rider.

PART 4

Identity

Self-awareness is at the core of identity. It's the lens through which we see ourselves and the world around us. The more self-aware we are, the better equipped we become at understanding our motivations, actions, and emotions. Without self-awareness, we drift through life reacting to situations rather than consciously choosing how to respond.

When it comes to identity, self-awareness isn't about navel-gazing or overanalyzing every thought and feeling. It's about being in tune with your strengths, weaknesses, and values. Everything that makes you who you are. It's about recognizing the stories you tell yourself and others about who you are and also knowing when those stories are true and when they're just excuses or rationalizations.

In the Code of the West, self-awareness is the foundation for personal responsibility. Cowboys, in their solitude and often harsh environments, had little choice but to confront themselves. There's no running from who you are when you're out on the range, miles from civilization. That self-awareness became crucial to survival, not just in the physical sense but in terms of maintaining integrity and purpose.

One of the challenges of modern life is that it's easy to lose touch with who we are. With constant distractions from technology and media, many people never take the time to reflect on their own thoughts and actions. But cultivating self-awareness is a powerful tool for reclaiming your sense of self. When you understand yourself on a deeper level, you're able to navigate the world with more confidence, make better decisions, and live more authentically.

Self-awareness also extends to understanding how you affect the people around you. It's not just about introspection but about being mindful of how your actions impact your community. A self-aware person can see beyond their own needs and recognize their place within a larger framework. This kind of awareness builds stronger connections with others and fosters a sense of belonging and purpose.

In a world that often encourages superficiality, true self-awareness sets you apart. It's a quiet strength that allows you to stay grounded, no matter how much the world around you changes. By cultivating this awareness, you lay the groundwork for a life lived with intention and integrity.

VALUES AND BELIEFS
The Compass for Identity

Values and beliefs are the foundation of who we are. They shape how we see the world, how we interact with others, and, most important, how we see ourselves. These internal guiding principles are deeply personal, yet they are also influenced by elements of our environment like our upbringing, our community, and our experiences. In the context of the Code of the West, values such as honor, integrity, and loyalty have long been upheld as cornerstones of personal and communal identity.

To understand values, it's essential to first recognize that they are not static. We can evolve as we grow, face new challenges, and learn from our mistakes. What we value in our younger years may shift dramatically as we age, experience loss, or gain wisdom. This is where the importance of resilience comes in, as maintaining your core values in the face of adversity is often a true test of character.

Why are values so important to identity?

Because they act as your moral compass. They guide your decisions, shape your relationships, and define your role in your community. Without a clear set of values, it's easy to lose your way, falling victim to external pressures or trends that don't align with who you truly are.

Beliefs, on the other hand, are often the frameworks we use to make sense of the world. While beliefs can be influenced by religion, philosophy, or personal experiences, they are the lens through which we interpret life. Just like values, beliefs can change over time, especially as we encounter new information or face significant life events. But the core of these beliefs, like what you fundamentally believe about yourself and the world, can serve as a stabilizing force, helping you stay grounded when life becomes unpredictable.

The key to a strong identity is alignment. When your actions reflect your values and beliefs, you move through the world with a sense of purpose and confidence. Disconnection from these principles often results in confusion, frustration, or a sense of aimlessness. But when you're in harmony with your beliefs, you create a consistent and authentic version of yourself—someone others can trust and someone you can be proud to be.

COMMUNITY

The Power and Pitfalls of Belonging

Community is often seen as one of the strongest sources of identity. It's where we find connection, support, and a sense of belonging.

But being part of a community doesn't just shape who you are. The relationships present there challenge you to understand where you fit within a larger group, and it tests your ability to balance individuality with collective needs. At its best, community brings out our highest values, like loyalty, kindness, and cooperation. At its worst, it can enforce conformity and stifle personal growth.

The role of community in identity isn't just about fitting in; it's about how you navigate the expectations of the group while staying true to yourself. Sometimes, the most difficult challenges come not from external forces but from the internal pressures of being part of something bigger than yourself. How do you maintain your own sense of self when the community pushes you in a different direction?

A community is powerful because it offers a shared identity and a collective strength, but that strength can come at a price if you're not careful. It's easy to lose your individuality when trying to please others or when you're drawn too deep into the group mentality.

When this happens, people can lose sight of their own values, allowing the group to dictate their decisions.

But a healthy relationship with community does the opposite. It doesn't mean losing yourself. The goal is to find balance within it, not to lose yourself to it. It's about contributing to something larger while keeping your own compass intact. A strong individual makes the community *stronger,* just as a supportive community helps individuals grow. This is the relationship that builds a resilient and adaptable society.

Finding your place in a community is one of the greatest gifts and challenges of personal identity. It requires self-awareness and the courage to assert your values, even when the group pulls in a different direction. The right community pushes you to grow while respecting your autonomy. It's not about suppressing your identity but about enriching it through shared purpose and connection.

SELF-REFLECTION VS. SELF-CRITICISM

The Balance of Growth

One of the most important elements of developing a strong sense of identity is learning how to evaluate yourself honestly. But there's a fine line between self-reflection and self-criticism, and knowing the difference can shape whether you grow from your experiences or become stuck in a cycle of negativity.

Self-reflection is a tool for growth. It's about looking inward with a clear and compassionate mindset, recognizing your strengths and areas that need improvement, and using that knowledge to move forward. It's not about ignoring your mistakes but about understanding them and seeing them as opportunities to learn. Reflection allows you to connect the dots between your actions and their consequences without the weight of harsh judgment. It's a practice of accountability without self-punishment.

Self-criticism, on the other hand, is a trap. It's when reflection turns into an internal dialogue of blame, shame, and negativity. Rather than focusing on growth, self-criticism focuses on tearing yourself down for your perceived shortcomings. It's a voice that dwells on failure and prevents you from seeing your potential for improvement. When self-criticism takes over, it becomes hard to see a way forward and even harder to believe in your own ability to grow.

In the Code of the West, resilience and self-awareness are key. Self-reflection fits into that because it helps you recognize where you are, where you've been, and where you need to go next. But to make that reflection productive, it has to come from a place of self-respect. You can't improve what you don't understand, and you can't understand what you only criticize.

The goal is to strike a balance—acknowledge your flaws without letting them define you and use self-reflection as a tool to shape a stronger, more resilient identity.

PERSONAL RESPONSIBILITY

Owning Your Life

Personal responsibility is at the heart of identity. It's about recognizing that, while we can't control everything that happens to us, we are responsible for how we respond to life's challenges, for the choices we make, and for the actions we take. It's about taking ownership of our own lives (both the victories and the failures) without blaming external factors or looking for excuses.

In a world that often rewards deflection and passes off blame, personal responsibility stands as a cornerstone of character. It's not just about avoiding excuses but about embracing accountability. The decisions we make, the way we interact with others, and how we handle both success and failure are all reflections of our true self.

To own your own identity fully, you must accept that your actions ripple outward, affecting not just yourself but the community and world around you.

This sense of responsibility is deeply tied to the Code of the West. Historically, in the untamed territories of the American frontier, a person had to rely on their own integrity and actions to get by.

If they didn't own their word, their work, or their decisions, they couldn't expect to earn the trust and respect of others. In those times, it was understood: You are the sum of what you do.

Personal responsibility also feeds into self-awareness. It's not enough to just know who you are; you have to act on that knowledge. Understanding your strengths, your weaknesses, and your values means nothing if you don't take responsibility for living in accordance with them. There's a saying: "You are what you repeatedly do." This couldn't be truer when it comes to owning your life and the decisions that shape it.

True personal responsibility requires humility. It means owning up to mistakes, learning from them, and making changes. It's easy to take credit when things go well, but real growth happens when we face our failures and recognize where we've fallen short. It's not about perfection but about progress. And the more accountable we become, the more capable we are of forging a strong, authentic identity.

AUTHENTICITY AND INTEGRITY

Living Your Values

Authenticity and integrity aren't just words we throw around; they're the backbone of living a life that's true to who you are. But in a world where distractions, pressures, and outside influences are constant, staying true to your values is often easier said than done. It's the challenge of living in the real world while keeping a firm hold on the internal compass that guides you.

To be authentic means to know yourself, your beliefs, and your principles and to live according to them. This isn't about perfection. It's about consistency. It's about making sure that your actions reflect the values you hold dear, even when the easier path would be to compromise.

In his collection of writings, *Meditations,* Marcus Aurelius talks about living in accordance with nature, both the nature of the world and the nature of oneself. The essence of this teaching is that while we can't control everything outside of us, we can control our response to it. When you know who you are and what you stand for, the external world becomes something you navigate with clarity rather than something that defines you.

But it takes integrity to keep that balance. Integrity is what keeps you grounded when life presents temptations to stray from your values. It's the quiet commitment to doing what's right, even when no one is watching. It's also about holding yourself accountable when you do falter, because no one gets it right all the time.

The important part is coming back to center. To live authentically with integrity means that when you're tested by people, circumstances, or even your own weaknesses, you hold fast to the principles you've set for yourself. You may bend, but you don't break. That's where the strength of identity really shows itself: in staying true to who you are, no matter how hard the world pushes against you.

This section of identity ties directly to everything we've explored so far: purpose, resilience, and self-awareness. Just as purpose gives you direction and resilience helps you face adversity, authenticity and integrity ensure that the path you walk is genuinely your own. It's how you take responsibility for not just what you do but who you are.

STAYING TRUE TO YOUR NORTH STAR

Living Your Own Narrative

When I moved to New York to pursue my dream of becoming a comic book artist, I had a clear plan in mind. I wanted to learn the craft, work with the best, and get my career off the ground. Part of that plan involved working as an assistant to Paul Pope, one of the most respected cartoonists in the field. It was everything I had hoped for.

But then something unexpected happened. I was offered a job helping to open a new Filson store in the city. Filson, a company from Seattle, was close to my heart. I'd worn their clothes while working in the mountains, and their gear symbolized a rugged, hardworking lifestyle I admired. I thought, "Why not introduce these people to a piece of my world?"

What I didn't expect was the backlash from people back home. They couldn't understand why I would take a retail job when I was in New York to chase my dreams. It seemed to them like I was abandoning my path. To them, the narrative was supposed to be linear: Go to New York, work in comics, achieve success. But life rarely follows such a straight line.

Taking that Filson job wasn't a deviation—it was part of my journey, even though others couldn't see it. The people who criticized my decision weren't trying to hold me back; they just couldn't reconcile it with the story they thought I should be living. But here's the thing: It wasn't their story. It was mine.

And as it turned out, taking that job set off a chain of events that completely shaped my future. Working with Filson led to consulting opportunities, which eventually led me to Black Rifle Coffee Company. Black Rifle is a creative-led, veteran-founded coffee company some of you may know. It was there that I had the chance to put all the skills I'd been unknowingly collecting together for the first time, and from that synthesis came the confidence to create Code of the West. If I had listened to the well-intentioned voices telling me to stay on the "right" path, my life would have been very different and not necessarily better.

Staying true to your North Star means listening to your own intuition and principles, even when others don't understand. It's about trusting that the steps you're taking, no matter how unconventional, are leading you somewhere meaningful. Your narrative is your own, and only you can decide how it unfolds.

PURPOSE AND IDENTITY
The Evolving Journey

When we set out with a purpose in mind, especially a purpose tied closely to our identity, it's easy to become fixated on a specific outcome. We think achieving a particular goal will fulfill us, that once we reach the top of the mountain, everything will click into place. But what happens when we get there and the view isn't quite what we imagined?

Take my story, for example. I moved to New York to pursue my dream of becoming a comic book writer and artist. It was a goal I'd had since I was ten years old, and it became the purpose that shaped my entire identity. I worked hard, studied with a master, and eventually published my first graphic novel. I even won an award for it. From the outside, it looked like I had achieved everything I set out to do.

But the reality was different. After reaching the top, I found that the dream I had been chasing for so long didn't bring the fulfillment I thought it would. I was struggling to get jobs, and the industry around me was shifting. For years, my identity was wrapped so tightly around this singular purpose that it became difficult to imagine a different path. I felt like I had lost my sense of direction.

It took stepping back and reevaluating my life to realize that I had been too narrowly defining my purpose. I had attached my identity to the idea of being a comic book creator, but what I was really chasing all along was storytelling. Once I understood that, my world opened up. I walked away from comics and embraced the broader identity of a storyteller. And that's when I found new opportunities—working with brands like Filson and Black Rifle and starting Code of the West. I had unlocked a more three-dimensional version of my purpose.

I hope this story serves as a reminder that our purpose, while important, should never be rigid. It should evolve as we do. Sometimes, what we think is the destination is really just a milestone along the way to something deeper. Our identity is not bound by a single goal; it's shaped by how we grow and adapt as life changes around us.

Purpose, when understood in this way, becomes an anchor, not a cage. It gives us direction but leaves room for flexibility. It allows us to embrace new opportunities without losing sight of the core values that drive us forward. That's where real personal growth happens—when we realize that our identity isn't about reaching one specific destination but about navigating the journey with resilience, adaptability, and an open heart.

RESILIENCE AND IDENTITY

Weathering the Storm of Self

In many ways, resilience is the foundation of identity. Who you are isn't defined by the easy days that go as planned. It's shaped by how you face the unpredictable storms.

In building Code of the West, I had to learn this the hard way. While Code of the West was an idea that captured a sense of America's shared story, I quickly realized that telling that story required a kind of resilience that I hadn't fully anticipated.

When I left Black Rifle and was a year and a half into Code of the West, I hit a wall. I wasn't living up to what I was espousing in the tenets of the Code. I realized that I had to step back. Not from my vision but from the business side of things. I had to rebuild myself in alignment with the code I was preaching.

I wasn't just weathering the external challenges of business; I was weathering an internal storm. My identity, tethered to this idea of Code of the West, needed to be strengthened. Resilience wasn't just about pushing forward—it was about the ability to adapt and grow stronger, mentally and emotionally, through those challenges.

In order to truly live out the Code of the West, I had to reflect deeply on my own habits, my health, and my mindset. This wasn't just about surviving setbacks but about becoming the kind of person who can thrive despite them. I had to become more than just a man running a brand. I had to become a man who could live the values of that brand, who could stand tall in the face of uncertainty, and who could use the storms to become stronger.

Building yourself through these challenges is the key to building a true and lasting identity. It's the process of integrating resilience into who you are, so that when life throws obstacles your way, you aren't just reacting—you're evolving.

Resilience, in the end, isn't about bouncing back. It's about getting back on the horse with a stronger sense of purpose and a clearer idea of who you are. Every challenge is a chance to refine your identity, to ensure that it's not only resilient in the face of adversity but thriving because of it.

IDENTITY AND THE TRANSITION TO COMMUNITY

As we've explored, identity is more than just who we are as individuals. It's about the principles we live by, the challenges we face, and the purpose we discover along the way. By building a strong sense of identity rooted in self-awareness, resilience, and a clear sense of purpose, we lay the groundwork for how we show up in the world.

But no identity is fully formed in isolation. The next step, and perhaps the most important, is how this identity extends outward and how it influences the communities we are part of. A strong personal identity isn't just a reflection of who we are on the inside; it's also a force that shapes the world around us.

As we transition from identity to community, it's important to recognize that the strength of a community lies in the integrity and resilience of its individuals. When we show up with purpose and authenticity, we contribute to something larger than ourselves. This is where the tenets of the Code of the West come full circle. Our actions, guided by our principles, don't just define who we are; they shape the kind of communities we help to build.

The road to building a better future, whether for our families, our neighborhoods, or our country, begins with individuals who are committed to living with intention. By embracing the values that define us, we create ripples that extend far beyond our personal lives. And as we'll explore in the next section, it's through the strength of these individual ripples that we can transform the collective tide of our communities.

PART 5

Community

Community is more than just the people around you; it's the interconnected web of individuals who influence, support, and challenge each other. While identity and purpose shape the individual, community is the environment where those traits are put to the test.

It's where we see the ripple effects of personal responsibility and resilience played out in real time. A strong community is not built through rules or mandates but through a shared sense of responsibility, mutual respect, and trust.

At the heart of this is the idea that a community thrives when individuals take accountability for themselves and work in alignment with the principles of the larger group. But this doesn't mean sacrificing individuality. Rather, it's about understanding that by being your best self, you contribute to the greater good. When people come together with a common understanding of values, like the tenets of the Code of the West, it creates an ecosystem where both personal growth and collective success can flourish.

True community, then, isn't just about being part of a group for the sake of it. It's about individuals who bring their strengths and principles into a shared space where everyone benefits from the collective progress.

Community isn't just a collection of individuals; it's the sum of shared values, actions, and responsibilities. When individuals live by a personal code rooted in purpose and resilience, they naturally contribute to a stronger, healthier society. In this section, we'll explore how the personal aligns with the collective, how individual integrity shapes communal well-being, and how being part of a community can inspire each of us to live a more fulfilled, purposeful life.

From the neighborhoods we live in to the nation we call home, the strength of any community depends on the character of its people. And as we'll see, the key to thriving as a community is rooted in the same principles that guide us as individuals. Principles such as responsibility, trust, and mutual respect. Let's start with the foundation: the power of individual action within a community.

INDIVIDUAL ACTION AND THE RIPPLE EFFECT IN COMMUNITY

At the heart of any thriving community is the power of individual action. It's easy to think that one person's contribution doesn't make a difference, but that couldn't be further from the truth. Communities are built on the collective efforts of individuals, each contributing their unique strengths, values, and ideas. When we take responsibility for our actions and lead by example, we create a ripple effect that influences those around us, and the way that ripple spreads can shape the entire community.

In the Code of the West, individual responsibility isn't just about personal success. We must also understand that our actions impact those around us. The cowboy on the range doesn't wait for someone else to step up when there's work to be done. He knows that taking initiative isn't just about self-reliance but also about setting a standard for those who follow. The ripple starts with one person and grows as others see the impact of that action, becoming inspired to take initiative themselves.

That ripple effect doesn't just mean that others are simply following suit; it's the beginning of a domino effect that changes the culture of a community. When each person commits to showing up with integrity and purpose, those values tend to spread. And as more people begin to see that, they adopt those principles as part of their own personal identity. The values you live by set the tone for what becomes acceptable, desirable, and honorable within the community. In this way, your personal actions become the bedrock upon which a larger shared ethos is built.

Individual action also fosters a sense of ownership and personal investment. When you understand that your efforts contribute to something larger than yourself, it creates a sense of pride and belonging. This sense of ownership leads to deeper engagement because you no longer view the community as something outside yourself. Rather, you start to see how you're a vital part of its heartbeat. That personal investment encourages everyone to care about outcomes, and this shared responsibility strengthens the ties between individuals, making the community resilient.

In a world where we are increasingly disconnected, the ripple effect of individual action offers a way back to authentic community building. By taking ownership of our actions and understanding the broader impact of our decisions, we're not just helping ourselves but ensuring that the people around us rise up as well. And when each person does that, the entire community thrives, rooted in the actions of individuals who understand their role in the bigger picture.

SHARED RESPONSIBILITY AND MUTUAL BENEFIT

In a community, responsibility is not a zero-sum game. When one person steps up and takes responsibility, it doesn't diminish the need for others to do the same; it magnifies it. The strength of a community isn't just built on the actions of one leader or a few individuals; it thrives when responsibility is shared across the board. When every person recognizes their role in maintaining the health, vitality, and integrity of the group, the community becomes something greater than the sum of its parts.

Shared responsibility fosters a mutual benefit. When each person takes ownership of their part, everyone benefits from the collective effort. It's the recognition that no one can do it all alone. The cowboy understands that even though he may be riding solo for a stretch, his work feeds into the larger efforts of the ranch, the cattle drive, or the community. His success is intertwined with the success of others. Likewise, when a rancher builds a fence, it doesn't just protect one cow but rather the entire herd.

The same applies to the values and principles we live by. When you live with integrity and take responsibility, it strengthens the moral fabric of the community. When everyone contributes their part, the whole becomes more resilient, more adaptable, and more able to weather the storms that inevitably come. Shared responsibility doesn't just lighten the load; it ensures that no one is left carrying the burden alone. It's a safeguard against burnout and a way of ensuring that the community stays strong, even when faced with challenges.

This mutual benefit is not about self-sacrifice but about understanding that by helping others, you help yourself. When you invest in the well-being of those around you, you create a community that can support you in return. It's not a system of obligation but one of opportunity. By taking responsibility and contributing to the group, you enhance your own well-being while ensuring the prosperity of the collective. This is the essence of shared responsibility within a social contract. It's a partnership where everyone plays a role and everyone stands to gain.

THE POWER OF INDIVIDUALITY WITHIN THE GROUP

One of the greatest strengths of any community lies in the individuality of its members. A thriving community isn't built by creating carbon copies of the same person but by embracing the unique talents, perspectives, and contributions that each individual brings. In the Code of the West, the cowboy is revered not just for his rugged independence but for how his individuality enriches the larger group. His ability to stand alone, to make decisions on his own, and to trust his instincts makes him a valuable asset to the community.

At first glance, individuality might seem at odds with the concept of community. How can a person prioritize their own uniqueness while contributing to a collective good? The answer lies in balance. A strong community shouldn't demand conformity. Instead it should ask for contribution. It should ask for the best of what you have to offer, without requiring you to erase your own identity in the process.

Think of a ranch: Each member of the team has a role to play, and those roles are distinct. One person might be great with horses, while another excels at managing the cattle. The success of the ranch doesn't come from everyone doing the same thing; it comes from everyone doing their best in their area of expertise. The individuality of each cowboy feeds into the strength of the whole, and the community thrives because of these differences, not in spite of them.

When individuality is respected and allowed to flourish, the community becomes stronger, more innovative, and more resilient. Different perspectives offer different solutions to problems, and unique skills allow for a more dynamic approach to challenges. This diversity of thought and ability is what makes a community adaptable.

It's why when faced with adversity, a community that respects the individuality of its members can pivot more easily and find creative ways through challenges that a homogenous group might miss.

But it's important to note that individuality doesn't mean going rogue. In the context of the Code, individuality is tied to responsibility. Your freedom to be yourself is balanced by your obligation to the group. When everyone is contributing their best selves, the whole is greater than the sum of its parts. But when individuality is used as an excuse to avoid responsibility, the community suffers. True individuality in a community is about finding the harmony between personal expression and group contribution.

In this way, a community built on the Code of the West encourages each person to be fully themselves while also ensuring that their unique gifts are used for the good of all. It's not about subsuming your identity. It's about finding how your identity can enhance the whole of the community and, in turn, how the community can support you in becoming the best version of yourself.

TRUST AND ACCOUNTABILITY
The Bedrock of Community

In any community, trust is the foundation upon which everything else is built. Without trust, there's no collaboration, no support, and no growth. But trust doesn't come easily, nor should it. Trust has to be earned, and it has to be maintained. In the Code of the West, trust is forged through accountability. Every member of the community is responsible not just for themselves but for the people around them. This mutual accountability creates a bond that strengthens the entire group.

At its core, accountability is about being reliable. It's about doing what you say you're going to do, even when it's hard. It's about showing up when you're needed and being honest when you've made a mistake. Trust grows when people can count on each other to follow through, to be transparent, and to hold themselves to a high standard. The more people uphold this principle, the stronger the community becomes.

Accountability also means holding others accountable in a constructive way. It's not about looking for opportunities to criticize or tear someone down. Instead, it's about supporting each other in becoming better. When a member of the community falls short or strays from the values of the group, accountability means stepping in. Not to judge but to guide. A strong community doesn't let its members fail without offering them a chance to correct course. This doesn't mean enabling bad behavior, but it does mean giving people the opportunity to live up to their potential.

Trust and accountability are inseparable. You can't have one without the other. Trust is built through accountability, and accountability is made meaningful by the trust that it fosters. When people know that their actions matter, not just to themselves but to the group, they take their responsibilities more seriously. And when others see that commitment, they're more likely to trust in the strength of the community.

One of the key aspects of accountability is that it's reciprocal. In a community that follows the Code of the West, you're not just responsible for others. They're responsible for you as well. This creates a system of checks and balances that keeps everyone on track. When someone stumbles, they can rely on the support of the group to get back up. And when the group faces a challenge, it can rely on the individuals within it to step up.

But trust isn't static. It's a living, breathing thing that has to be nurtured and reinforced over time. Every interaction, every decision, every moment of accountability, either strengthens or weakens the trust within the community. This is why it's crucial to treat trust as the precious resource it is. In the same way that a rancher tends to the land to ensure that it remains fertile, members of a community must tend to the trust they've built, making sure it continues to grow.

Trust and accountability aren't just ideals to strive for. Rather, they're practical necessities for any thriving community. When people hold each other accountable with respect and integrity, they build something far stronger than any individual effort could ever achieve.

They build a community that can stand the test of time.

SHARED VALUES

The Glue That Holds Communities Together

Communities thrive on shared values. Without them, a group is just a collection of individuals pursuing their own interests. Shared values give the community a sense of purpose and direction, helping everyone stay aligned even when challenges arise. In the Code of the West, these values form the core of what binds people together, creating a unified sense of identity and belonging.

Shared values have to be cultivated. They come from the collective experiences of the group, the lessons learned through hard work, adversity, and triumph. The values that emerge are the ones that have proven themselves time and time again to be essential for survival and success. In the Old West, values like integrity, loyalty, and self-reliance were not just ideals. They were functional necessities for life on the frontier. And while the world has changed, those core values remain just as relevant today.

One of the reasons why shared values are so powerful is that they provide a common language for the community. When everyone understands what's important, it becomes easier to navigate disagreements, solve problems, and work toward a common goal. Shared values give people something bigger than themselves to believe in, which is vital in keeping the community strong.

It's important to remember, though, that shared values don't mean uniformity. In fact, diversity of thought and experience can strengthen a community by bringing new perspectives to old problems. But what keeps that diversity from fragmenting the group is the shared commitment to certain foundational principles. These principles act as a compass, guiding the community even as individuals take different paths to reach their goals.

Shared values also serve as a safety net. When times get tough, people lean on those values to guide them through. They provide stability in an unstable world, reminding everyone of what really matters. Whether it's honoring commitments, helping a neighbor in need, or showing respect to others, shared values give the community a sense of continuity and trust that endures, no matter what storms come their way.

At the heart of shared values is the idea that you're part of something larger than yourself. In a world that often emphasizes individualism to the point of isolation, shared values remind us that we're all interconnected. The success of the community is tied to the success of the individual, and vice versa. By upholding the values that matter, everyone contributes to the strength and well-being of the whole.

Shared values aren't just about tradition, either. Social mores and dogmas don't just spontaneously sprout up. They evolve as a community grows. As new challenges arise, the community must adapt and sometimes reevaluate which values are most important. This doesn't mean abandoning the core principles that define the group, but it does mean being open to refining how those values are applied in a changing world. A community rooted in shared values is resilient precisely because it knows what to hold on to and what to let go of.

Ultimately, shared values are the glue that holds communities together. They create a sense of belonging, purpose, and direction that keeps people aligned, even in the face of adversity. And while the world may change, those values serve as a constant reminder of what's important, not just for the individual but for the community as a whole.

The principles that hold a community together, such as shared values, personal responsibility, and mutual respect, don't just apply to small groups, either. They can scale to something much larger, like a state, a nation, or even a country.

America, at its best, is built on the same foundation as any strong community. At its heart, the American experiment is about finding unity in diversity through shared ideals.

When you look at America through the lens of the Code of the West, it's clear that the values that make a good cowboy are the same values that can make a strong nation. Integrity, hard work, resilience, and respect for others are not just personal virtues but the building blocks of a healthy society. When these values are embraced at the community level, they radiate outward, influencing the larger fabric of the country.

In many ways, America is just a larger community. An enormous, diverse one, to be sure, but one still bound together by a set of shared ideals. The Constitution, the Bill of Rights, and the principles laid out by the Founding Fathers were designed to create a framework that allows individuals to thrive while contributing to the collective well-being. The idea of America has always been about balancing personal freedom with a commitment to the greater good.

However, just like in a small community, those shared values can't be taken for granted. They have to be nurtured and reinforced by individuals who believe in them. When people stop believing in the core values that built America, when they lose sight of what connects them, the sense of national community weakens. That's why it's important to constantly work at it, to recommit to those values every day in small, individual ways. It starts with how you live your life, how you interact with those around you, and how you show up for the people in your community.

Scaling shared values from the local to the national level also means acknowledging that we won't always agree on everything. America's strength comes not from uniformity but from the ability to find common ground in the midst of diversity. Just like in a small town, where people may have different ways of thinking but still come together for the greater good, the same can be true for the nation.

It's about remembering that, despite our differences, we're all part of something bigger. Something worth preserving and nurturing.

One of the key lessons of the Code of the West is that you take responsibility not just for yourself but for those around you. This same principle applies to the country as a whole. It's not enough to focus solely on personal success or individual freedom. There's a duty to contribute to the well-being of the community at large, and in America's case, that community is massive, diverse, and ever-changing. But the core values that hold it together—respect, resilience, and personal integrity—remain the same.

The Code of the West doesn't just teach us how to be better individuals. It shows us how to build better communities and, ultimately, how to contribute to a stronger America. When individuals live by these values, they naturally influence those around them. Their communities become more resilient, more cohesive, and more capable of weathering the challenges ahead. And when communities are strong, the country itself becomes stronger.

At the end of the day, America is only as strong as the communities that make it up. If we want to see the country live up to its ideals, we have to start by living those ideals ourselves. That's how the values that built the West can help rebuild America. One person, one community, and one shared principle at a time.

CONTRIBUTION AND PARTICIPATION

Everyone Has a Role

In any functioning community, no matter how big or small, there's one undeniable truth: Every individual plays a role. It might be tempting to think that some people's contributions matter more than others. Like those in leadership roles, for example, or those with specialized skills. But the reality is that a community thrives only when everyone participates, regardless of their role or status.

When you think about how a small town survives in tough conditions, it's not just the mayor or the business owners who keep things running. It's the teachers, the farmers, the tradespeople, and the countless others who, day by day, ensure that life continues. The key is that contribution isn't about grand gestures; it's about consistently showing up.

In the context of the Code of the West, participation is nonnegotiable. You don't ride alone in life; your actions, your integrity, and your effort impact those around you. Even the smallest contribution can make a world of difference. Whether it's offering a helping hand or simply living by example, your presence shapes the health and strength of the community.

But it's more than just participating. It's about doing so with intention and purpose. It's not enough to just show up. True contribution requires putting something of yourself into the task. Your effort, your expertise, your energy are where individual purpose intersects with community. When you contribute to your community, you're not just fulfilling an obligation; you're reinforcing the very values that make your community worth being a part of.

In modern society, we often see people become passive participants watching from the sidelines rather than actively engaging. It's easy to sit back and assume that someone else will take care of the heavy lifting. But that's not how strong communities are built. Every person, regardless of their role, has a responsibility to engage, to participate, and to contribute.

It's also worth noting that participation isn't just about tangible work. It's about showing up emotionally and mentally, supporting those around you, and helping foster an environment where others feel valued and motivated to contribute as well. It's about stepping in when help is needed and stepping back when it's time for others to lead.

The stronger the individual, the stronger the community. And the more engaged each person is, the healthier the community becomes. The Code of the West reminds us that participation is essential not because it's easy but because it's necessary. In a world that often encourages isolation and individualism, choosing to contribute is a radical act of community building.

COLLABORATION AND COOPERATION

The Power of Working Together

For a community to thrive, the necessity of collaboration and cooperation cannot be understated. The individual can be strong, yes, but when people come together with shared goals, the potential for impact grows exponentially. This is the bedrock of what makes communities resilient and prosperous. When people pool their talents, resources, and efforts, they can achieve far more than any one person working alone.

This principle is rooted in the very foundation of human survival. Throughout history, humans have banded together for protection, for trade, and for progress. The same idea applies today, whether it's a small-town community rallying around a local business or a nation coming together during a crisis. When individuals choose to collaborate rather than compete, they generate a force that can drive meaningful change and success.

Collaboration doesn't mean sacrificing personal identity or independence; rather, it strengthens the individual by creating a network of support. Just as we've discussed the importance of personal resilience, the resilience of a community is built on the interdependence of its members. Everyone brings their unique strengths to the table, and when those strengths are combined, the community as a whole becomes stronger, more adaptable, and better equipped to handle challenges.

However, collaboration is not without its challenges. It requires clear communication, trust, and a willingness to compromise when necessary. This is where cooperation comes into play. Cooperation is the practical application of collaboration. It's the day-to-day work of aligning efforts, solving problems, and moving forward together. It's easy to agree on a shared goal or a desired outcome, but the real test of a community's strength is found in its ability to cooperate when things get difficult.

The key to successful cooperation is mutual respect and a recognition that everyone in the community plays a role. Whether someone is a leader or a follower, everyone's contribution is valuable. In fact, some of the strongest communities are those where leadership is dynamic—people who step up when needed and step back when it's someone else's time to lead.

By fostering a culture of collaboration and cooperation, communities are able to turn effort into effective change. This is the engine that powers innovation, growth, and lasting change. It's also the foundation of a strong and united society, where individuals are empowered to contribute and everyone benefits from the collective effort.

THE ROLE OF LEADERSHIP IN A COMMUNITY

Leadership is often seen as a position of power, but in a healthy community, it's more about responsibility than authority. The best leaders are those who understand that their role is to serve their community, not to dominate it. True leadership is about empowering others, guiding with integrity, and being a model for the values that the community stands for.

In the context of the Code of the West, leadership takes on a unique form. It's not about titles or rank; it's about character and action. In the old West, leaders were often chosen by their deeds. Those who lived by the code, upheld fairness, and led by example earned the respect of those around them. This is the kind of leadership that creates lasting bonds and a strong sense of trust within a community.

Effective leaders understand that their strength comes from the people they serve. They know that without the trust and cooperation of the community, their influence is limited. That's why humility is a key component of leadership. A good leader knows they don't have all the answers and is willing to listen, learn, and adapt. They recognize the value in the perspectives of others and foster an environment where people feel heard and respected.

Another essential trait of strong leadership is determination. Leading a community is not without challenges, and it's in these difficult times that true leaders show their worth. Whether it's navigating a crisis, making tough decisions, or guiding the community through change, a leader's ability to stay calm, focused, and solution oriented sets the tone for everyone else. A leader who can weather the storm inspires confidence and trust.

Leadership in a community also requires a forward-thinking mindset. It's not enough to address the problems of today; leaders must anticipate the needs of tomorrow. They must be proactive, looking for ways to improve the community and prepare for future challenges. This kind of vision is what keeps a community growing and evolving.

Lastly, leadership isn't reserved for a select few. In a strong community, leadership is fluid. It's not about one person carrying the weight. It's integral to recognize that everyone has the potential to lead in different ways, whether it's by offering support, taking initiative, or stepping up when the moment calls for it. The best communities are those where leadership is shared and where everyone feels empowered to contribute.

When leadership is rooted in service, integrity, and resilience, it creates a community that is strong, adaptable, and ready to face whatever lies ahead. It fosters trust and cooperation, and it ensures that the community can thrive, even in challenging times.

TRUST
The Cornerstone of Leadership and Community

Trust is the foundation of any healthy relationship, community, or society. Without it, everything collapses—leadership falters, cooperation diminishes, and the sense of unity crumbles. Trust isn't just about words; it's about actions that consistently align with the values you claim to uphold. As the old adage goes: "Trust is hard to gain but easy to lose." And this is especially true when building communities or guiding others. Trust takes time to nurture and can vanish in a single moment of carelessness or dishonesty.

To build trust, you must show up with consistency, integrity, and a willingness to be vulnerable when needed. These qualities show others that you're reliable and that your word is good. In the Code of the West, one of the highest values is to "keep your word." This simple phrase embodies a lifetime of wisdom. A person's word is their bond, and every promise kept strengthens the foundation of trust.

In leadership, trust is not an accessory; it's essential. People don't follow those they don't trust. Leaders who are open, honest, and willing to take responsibility when things go wrong gain the respect of those they lead. They aren't seen just as managers or figureheads but as individuals willing to carry the weight of their decisions.

But what happens when that trust is broken? One misstep, one moment of hypocrisy, can undo years of careful work. Think of it as a structure built stone by stone. If the foundation cracks, the whole thing can come tumbling down. That's why, as leaders, we must be vigilant. We must guard against complacency and always strive to uphold the trust we've worked so hard to build.

Trust isn't only a matter of leadership; it's the glue that binds a community together. A community can be a family, a town, a workplace, or even an online collective. No matter the size or the context, trust is what holds it together.

When trust is present, people feel safe enough to speak openly, to collaborate, and to look out for one another. It's what makes individuals step up to protect the group, to help their neighbors, and to believe that their contributions matter. It's a quiet but powerful force that amplifies the effectiveness of any group effort.

But just like in leadership, when trust is broken, the effects ripple through the entire community. People grow cautious, defensive, and less willing to work together. Mistrust breeds division, and division weakens the whole.

Building trust requires more than a single gesture. It calls for continuous practice. It's in the small, everyday actions that trust grows. It's in showing up on time, keeping promises, admitting mistakes, and doing the right thing even when it's hard. The foundation of trust is laid in moments when no one is watching, but it becomes visible in how people respond to you when the chips are down.

To lead a community, to live by the Code of the West, is to recognize that trust is not given freely. It's earned, nurtured, and protected with care. It's a slow process, but it's the only way to build something lasting.

COMMUNITY

The Sum of Our Shared Efforts

A community is more than just a group of people living or working together. It's a living, breathing organism that thrives on the collective actions and attitudes of its members. Every individual, no matter their role, contributes to the health and vibrancy of the community. The Code of the West reminds us that we are not islands unto ourselves. Our actions, our choices, and our integrity all ripple outward, affecting everyone around us.

The strength of a community is built on shared values and a common understanding that we all have a responsibility to each other. When we live by principles like honor, resilience, and respect, we create an environment where everyone can thrive. But this isn't something that happens by accident. It's something we actively cultivate.

It starts with personal responsibility. Each person must take ownership of their actions, their words, and their contributions to the group. It's not about perfection; it's about accountability. When you do what you say you're going to do, when you show up for others, and when you act with integrity, you reinforce the fabric that holds the community together.

Personal responsibility also means recognizing that your success is not just your own; it's often intertwined with the success of those around you. In helping others succeed, you strengthen the whole. Whether it's offering a hand to someone in need or stepping up to mentor the next generation, these small acts of service create an environment where everyone has the opportunity to grow.

Shared values are what give a community its character. When everyone agrees on basic principles like honesty, kindness, hard work, and respect for others, the community becomes more than just a place to live or work. It becomes a reflection of its members' best selves. And when people live in alignment with those values, the community prospers.

But what happens when those values are challenged? How do we maintain a strong community when there's disagreement or when external pressures threaten to pull people apart? This is where resilience, both personal and collective, comes into play.

Communities, just like individuals, face adversity. Whether it's economic hardship, social unrest, or personal tragedy, these challenges can strain the bonds that hold us together. But strong communities, like strong people, don't break easily. They bend, adapt, and find ways to rebuild.

At its core, a community is a collaboration. It's the result of people coming together, recognizing their interdependence, and working toward a shared future. This is the promise of the Code of the West: that by living with purpose and integrity, by embracing personal responsibility, and by trusting in each other, we can create a future that's better than what came before.

Each generation has a choice. We can retreat into isolation, driven by self-interest and fear, or we can step up, take responsibility, and invest in the community around us. When we choose the latter, we create something lasting: a legacy that future generations can build upon.

In the end, community is the foundation upon which everything else rests. The strength of our society, our families, and our individual lives all stems from how well we work together, how deeply we trust one another, and how fully we live by the principles that guide us. The Code of the West may have started as a guide for survival in a harsh land, but today, it's a blueprint for building communities that endure.

As we close out this section on community, and the manual itself, take a moment to reflect on your own role. What can you do to strengthen the bonds around you? How can you contribute to the shared success of those in your life? It's easy to focus on personal goals and ambitions, but true fulfillment comes from knowing that your efforts have made a difference in the lives of others.

Live with intention. Act with honor. Trust in the power of community.

FINAL THOUGHTS
The Current State

The world we live in today is vastly different from what our grandparents and their grandparents knew. We have made incredible strides in technology, communication, and comfort, but somewhere along the way, we lost something critical. We lost our sense of a shared narrative, the one that used to tie us together with a common purpose. We became more connected than ever through screens yet more divided than we could have imagined in spirit.

This fragmentation isn't just a social issue; it affects each of us on a personal level. People feel lost, isolated, and uncertain about their place in the world. Purpose has been replaced by distraction, and community has been replaced by competition. The rules of the past, the unwritten codes that guided us, have faded into the background. We don't know where to look for guidance, and as a result, many of us drift.

But drifting is not our natural state. Human beings crave structure, meaning, and direction. This isn't just about base survival. More importantly, it's about thriving, about building a life of substance and purpose. That's why the principles behind the Code of the West are more relevant today than ever. They offer a blueprint for reclaiming a sense of order in a world that often feels chaotic.

The Code isn't about nostalgia for a past we can't return to. It's about rediscovering timeless values and applying them to modern life. It's about reminding ourselves that no matter how fast technology evolves, no matter how fragmented society becomes, certain truths remain the same. Honor, courage, and integrity aren't virtues that go in and out of style. They are the bedrock of any strong individual and, by extension, any strong community.

Living by the Code means reasserting personal responsibility. It means stepping up, not because it's easy or because there's a reward waiting but because it's necessary both for ourselves and for the people around us. In a time when we're more disconnected than ever, living with intention and purpose becomes a radical act. And that act starts with each individual choosing to live by a set of values that transcends the noise of the moment.

In today's world, it's easy to feel like we're adrift in an ocean of conflicting values. The narratives that once unified us are fractured, leaving behind a society that is more divided than ever. But the principles that underpin the Code aren't about forcing us all into one way of thinking. They're about offering a framework, a common ground on which we can stand while still retaining our individuality.

What we've lost, in many ways, is the myth that binds us. A shared story, something bigger than ourselves that we can aspire to. Without that, we've become increasingly isolated, focused on the individual to the detriment of the collective good. And that's where we've gone wrong. In pursuing personal success at all costs, we've neglected the responsibility we have to our communities, to the people around us.

This isn't a call to abandon self-interest; rather, it's about aligning our personal goals with the greater good. It's about recognizing that when we live with purpose and integrity, the ripple effects benefit not only ourselves but the world around us. When individuals thrive in a meaningful way, communities become stronger. When communities are strong, the fabric of the nation is reinforced. It's a simple truth but one we've lost sight of.

We need a way back. And that way starts with each of us choosing to live by a code. Not because it's convenient but because it's the right thing to do. Living by a code means accepting that your life has significance beyond your immediate desires. It's about recognizing that you're part of something larger, something worth contributing to.

At the heart of this entire manual is the power of choice. The truth is, no one can force you to live by a code. No one can dictate the path you take, the decisions you make, or the values you choose to uphold. But the real power lies in knowing that you can choose, and in that choice comes freedom.

Freedom doesn't come from doing whatever you want, whenever you want. That's a shallow version of liberty that ultimately leads to chaos. True freedom comes from living with intention, from setting a course for your life that is guided by purpose and principles. The kind of freedom we're talking about isn't about avoiding responsibility—it's about embracing it.

When you make the choice to live by the Code of the West, or by any set of guiding principles, you're not just accepting limits; you're creating structure. And within that structure, real growth and success can happen. You become stronger, more resilient, and more focused because you're not constantly at the whim of every passing desire or external force. You've grounded yourself in something that matters, something that can weather any storm.

But it's important to remember that this choice is ongoing. It's not something you do once and then forget about. Every day, you have the chance to recommit to living by the principles that guide you.

It's in the small daily decisions that you see the biggest impact over time. The power of choice, when wielded consistently and with purpose, has the potential to change not only your life but the lives of those around you.

The Code of the West isn't just about reading words on a page or nodding along with ideas that sound good. It's about taking these principles and applying them to your life, day in and day out.

We've laid out the pillars: purpose, resilience, identity, and community. We've talked about the importance of living with intention, of grounding yourself in something bigger than the moment, and of pushing forward even when the path is hard. But now it's your turn to act. To live the Code.

In a world that often pulls you toward distraction and quick fixes, there's real power in choosing to live by a set of values. You'll stand out, and you might even face resistance. But that's where the resilience we've talked about comes into play. You're not just building yourself; you're building something that will ripple out to those around you, to your community, and, ultimately, to your country.

The Code of the West represents an opportunity to recenter ourselves and reclaim what's been lost. It's not about going backward or romanticizing the past; it's about using timeless principles to navigate modern challenges. It's about acknowledging that while the world changes, some things stay constant—integrity, courage, respect, hard work. These are the values that can guide us forward.

As you step into your life, take the Code with you. Apply it in your relationships, in your work, in the way you interact with the world. This isn't just about you but about all of us. It's about the example you set for others. It's about the legacy you leave behind.

Remember: How you do anything is how you do everything. The way you choose to live by these principles, both in the big moments and in the small, is what will define your life and the impact you have. And in the end, that's what it's all about. Live the Code. Be the example.

Build a life and a world worth fighting for.

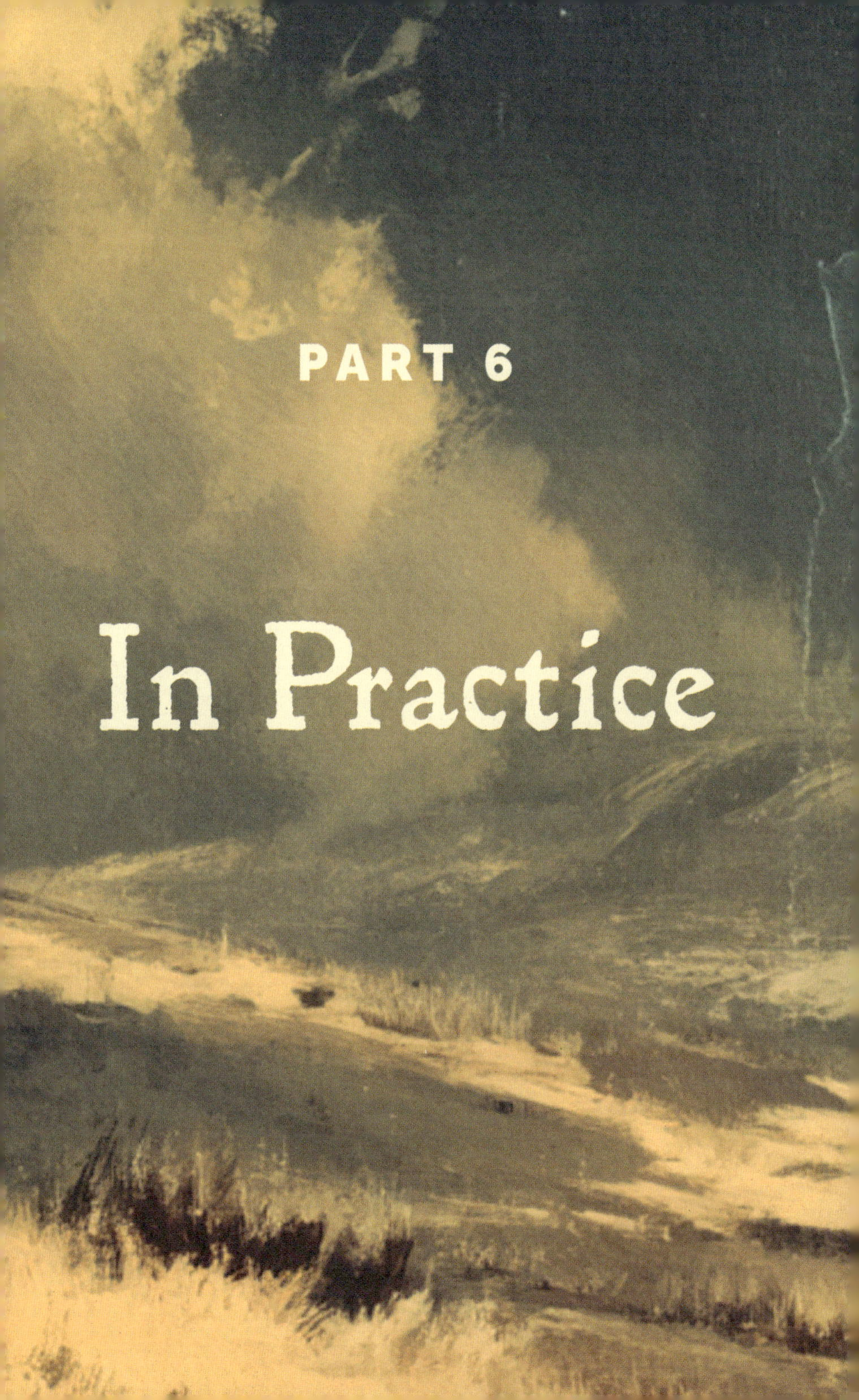

PART 6

In Practice

Social Media

SOCIAL MEDIA
Tool or Trap?

When social media platforms first emerged, they promised connection, community, and new ways to share our lives. What no one was prepared for was the seismic shift these platforms would create not just in how we communicate but in how we think, act, and relate to one another. Society as a whole had no blueprint or guideposts for how to navigate this new landscape.

Suddenly, we were more connected than ever, yet those connections were often shallow and fleeting. Social media became a tool, but without the right framework for using it, the tool began to shape us more than we shaped it. We weren't prepared for the relentless flood of information, the carefully curated images, or the way algorithms began to feed on our attention.

The platforms, designed to hold us captive, quickly evolved from a means of connection into something much more pervasive: a force that manipulates how we see the world and ourselves. Without any established understanding of how to engage with these platforms responsibly, many of us fell into patterns of addiction, comparison, and distraction, often without realizing it.

This lack of preparation is what we're now confronting, and it's why, as we move forward, it's crucial to recognize the impact that social media has had not just on communication but on our very way of thinking. To regain control, we need to understand that social media is not neutral. It has the potential to be either a powerful tool or a dangerous trap, depending on how we wield it.

Our task, then, is to take back control. Not by rejecting technology but by engaging with it consciously and with intention. Only by recognizing its influence can we begin to use it as a tool for good, rather than a trap that compromises our values and connections.

The choice, as with all things in life, is ours to make.

THE PSYCHOLOGY OF ATTENTION

In today's world, attention has become one of the most valuable commodities. Social media platforms are built around this very fact, with algorithms carefully designed to capture and keep our attention as long as possible. But the intent behind these systems isn't sinister; it's simply part of the business model. Platforms operate on engagement because the more time people spend interacting with content, the more successful the platform becomes.

These algorithms work by showing us things we're already likely to engage with, based on our behavior. They aren't inherently manipulative in a malicious sense; they're built to serve us content we find interesting. But the unintended result is that many of us find ourselves spending more time online than we anticipated, scrolling through endless streams of posts, videos, and stories.

What makes this so powerful is that these platforms tap into something deeper: the psychology of attention. Social media doesn't just offer content; it appeals to our most basic emotions. Posts that trigger joy, surprise, or even anger tend to keep us engaged longer, as they provoke strong reactions that feel rewarding. Over time, this creates a cycle of seeking out emotionally charged content, which leads to more prolonged interaction.

While the algorithms are optimized to keep us entertained, it's important to remember that they are also tuned to maximize our engagement, whether we're conscious of it or not. It's not that the platforms are evil; the real issue is that we, as users, have allowed ourselves to be guided by these systems. The platforms were designed to show us content we like, but in doing so, they shape our habits, often without us realizing it.

By understanding the way social media captures our attention, we can begin to recognize the patterns that keep us hooked. Awareness is the first step toward taking control. We don't need to reject social media, but we must engage with it deliberately, keeping in mind that our attention is precious and that how we spend it matters.

DOPAMINE AND THE REWARD CYCLE

At the core of social media's power is the way it taps into our brain's reward system. Every notification, like, or comment triggers the release of dopamine. Dopamine is a chemical that plays a key role in how we experience pleasure. This "hit" that dopamine provides is a brief feeling of satisfaction, which ends up reinforcing the behavior that led to it. Over time, this creates a cycle of reward-seeking behavior, where users return to social media again and again, chasing that fleeting sense of pleasure.

The platforms are designed to capitalize on this natural mechanism. While their goal is to keep us engaged by showing us content we enjoy, the unintended effect is that we become conditioned to seek out these rewards: constantly refreshing, checking, and scrolling in search of the next notification or like. Again, it's not that social media is inherently harmful, but the way it triggers our reward system can lead us into habits that are hard to break.

The more we engage with these platforms, the more our brains associate social media with rewards, creating a feedback loop that can be difficult to disrupt. It's a cycle that keeps us coming back for more, not because we consciously choose to but because we've been conditioned to expect the next dopamine rush. This is why we often find ourselves spending more time online than we intended, without even realizing it.

But there's power in understanding this process. Once we recognize the role that dopamine plays in our engagement with social media, we can start to break the cycle. By being more aware of how our brains respond to these platforms, we can regain control over how we spend our time online. It's not about rejecting technology but about using it with intention: knowing when to step away and prioritize real-world connections over fleeting digital rewards.

ECHO CHAMBERS AND REINFORCED BELIEFS

One of the unintended consequences of social media algorithms is the creation of echo chambers, which are environments where people are primarily exposed to information, opinions, and content that align with their existing beliefs. This happens because social media platforms are designed to keep users engaged, and one of the easiest ways to do that is by showing content that resonates with what users already like or agree with.

Over time, this leads to a narrowing of perspectives. Instead of encountering diverse viewpoints or being challenged to think critically, users are often fed a steady stream of content that reinforces their current beliefs. This can create the illusion that everyone around us thinks the same way, fostering a sense of certainty and even righteousness, but it also isolates us from the complexity and diversity of real-world views.

While the intent of these algorithms isn't to divide or polarize, the effect can be exactly that. By continually showing us content that reinforces what we already believe, we may become more entrenched in our views, less open to dialogue, and more resistant to new ideas. The echo chamber effect can make it difficult to find common ground with others, especially on important societal issues.

Awareness of this phenomenon is key. By recognizing the presence of echo chambers, we can make a conscious effort to seek out different perspectives, engage with challenging content, and critically evaluate the information we encounter online. The Code of the West teaches us to approach life with respect and integrity, which includes being open to understanding others—even when we don't agree with them. Breaking free from echo chambers is not about changing our beliefs but about maintaining the humility to learn and grow in a diverse world.

THE ILLUSION OF CONTROL

One of the most subtle aspects of social media is the illusion it creates: the illusion that we are fully in control of our experience. With features like personalized feeds, options to follow or unfollow accounts, and the ability to curate our content, it seems like we're in the driver's seat. But the reality is that much of what we see and engage with online is shaped by algorithms working behind the scenes, determining what appears in front of us.

At its core, an algorithm is a set of instructions or rules that a computer follows to solve a problem or make a decision. On social media, algorithms look at our behavior—what we like, share, or linger on—and use that information to predict what we'll want to see next. The goal is simple: to keep us engaged. But while it feels like we're choosing what content to interact with, the algorithm is actually filtering and prioritizing what gets shown to us, based on what it thinks will hold our attention the longest.

These algorithms are designed to predict our preferences based on our past behavior, showing us the content most likely to hold our attention. While this seems convenient, the result is that our engagement is subtly guided by these predictive systems, giving the appearance of choice while narrowing the actual range of content we see. Over time, this creates the illusion that we are fully in control, when in reality, many of our choices are influenced by forces we can't even see.

This illusion can lead to a sense of complacency. When we believe we're in control, we're less likely to question how the system works or to actively seek out content that challenges us. It's easy to believe that the information we consume is the result of our own decisions instead of recognizing the role the algorithms play in shaping those decisions.

Understanding this illusion is essential to regaining real control over our social media habits. The Code of the West values responsibility and awareness, traits that help us recognize when we're being led by outside forces and that empower us to take back the reins. By engaging with social media more consciously, we can make choices that align with our values rather than allow the algorithms to do the choosing for us.

REAL-LIFE CONNECTIONS

While social media promises to bring us closer together, the reality is that it often pulls us further apart. As we become more immersed in digital interactions and as we're commenting, liking, and scrolling, we may find that our real-life relationships suffer. Social media allows us to stay constantly connected, but this connection is often shallow, lacking the depth and nuance that comes from face-to-face interaction.

The more time we spend online, the less time we may devote to nurturing the relationships that matter most in our lives, like those with family, friends, and our communities. It's easy to fall into the trap of thinking that staying connected digitally is enough, but real-life relationships require time, attention, and presence—things that a quick comment or a double tap can't provide.

That said, it's important to recognize that genuine and authentic connections can still be fostered online. It just takes more intentional effort. While social media often encourages surface-level interaction, deeper connections can be made by engaging thoughtfully and with purpose. Just as in real life, meaningful online relationships require vulnerability, communication, and time.

Even so, digital interactions can sometimes create a sense of closeness without the effort that true relationships require. It's easier to present a curated version of ourselves online, one that doesn't require us to engage deeply or show our true selves. In this way, social media can create the illusion of connection while keeping us at a distance from real intimacy.

Recognizing this, it's important to prioritize real-world connections, especially when social media seems to consume more of our attention. The Code of the West values integrity and respect—qualities that are best cultivated through genuine relationships, built not only through digital platforms but also through shared experiences and meaningful conversations.

While social media has its place, we must ensure that it doesn't *replace* the deeper connections that give our lives purpose and meaning. By stepping away from the screen and investing in the people around us, we honor those relationships in ways that no algorithm ever could.

FINAL WORDS

The Disconnection from Reality

In a world where curated feeds and filtered images dominate, it's easy to lose sight of what's real. Social media presents a version of life that's often edited and polished, showing only the highlights, the successes, and the moments of perfection. This constant exposure to an idealized version of reality can leave us feeling inadequate or disconnected from our own lives. We see the best moments of others while comparing them to our own unfiltered reality, where life is messy, complicated, and far from perfect.

Over time, this disconnection from reality can impact our mental and emotional well-being. We may find ourselves striving for a version of success, beauty, or happiness that simply doesn't exist. The problem isn't just that social media presents a distorted view of reality but that we often internalize those images and start to believe that we're falling short. In truth, the lives we see online are carefully curated, often hiding the struggles and imperfections that are a natural part of being human.

Recognizing this disconnection is crucial for maintaining a balanced perspective. It's important to remember that what we see online is not the whole story but just a snapshot of someone's life—one that's often edited to look a certain way or to give a certain impression. The Code of the West teaches us to live with integrity and authenticity, embracing the reality of who we are rather than chasing a fictional version of life created for the screen.

By stepping back from the filtered world of social media, we can reconnect with the things that truly matter. Real life isn't perfect, and it's in our imperfections and struggles that we often find meaning and growth. Instead of measuring ourselves against the unrealistic standards of social media, we can find peace in accepting ourselves as we are—flaws and all. The more we embrace our own reality, the less we'll feel disconnected from it.

Leadership

LEADERSHIP WITHOUT AUTHORITY

True leadership isn't about holding a position of power or commanding a group of followers. It's about how you carry yourself through life. In the modern world, leadership is less about being the boss and more about the quiet strength that comes from walking your path with integrity and purpose. You don't need a title to lead; in fact, some of the most influential leaders are those who simply live by their values, regardless of whether anyone is watching.

Leadership without authority is about embodying the principles you believe in, no matter the circumstances. It's not about seeking validation or controlling others; it's about staying true to yourself and setting an example through your actions. When you lead this way, others may look to you for guidance not because you're telling them what to do but because you're showing them what it looks like to live with purpose and conviction.

This kind of leadership isn't flashy. It doesn't come with accolades or applause. It's about quiet diligence. Doing the right thing even when it's hard, even when no one else seems to notice. In a world that often rewards the loudest voices, real leaders are the ones who stand firm in their values, even when those values aren't popular.

At the heart of this approach is the idea that leadership is a way of being, not a position to hold. It's about being consistent, reliable, and true to your word. Whether you're interacting with coworkers, friends, or strangers, leadership is reflected in how you treat others and how you respond to the challenges that life throws your way.

QUIET DILIGENCE

In a world that often values noise and spectacle, true leadership can be found in the quiet moments of diligence. It's not about the loud proclamations or the grand gestures but rather the small, consistent actions that define who we are. Quiet diligence is the essence of leadership that doesn't seek attention but instead focuses on doing what's right even when no one is watching.

Quiet diligence is about showing up, day after day, and putting in the work, whether or not anyone notices. It's the discipline to stay true to your values when it would be easier to take shortcuts or follow the crowd. This kind of leadership doesn't rely on recognition; it thrives on integrity and a commitment to doing the right thing, even when it's difficult.

In today's fast-paced world, where instant gratification and constant feedback are the norm, quiet diligence is a form of leadership that's becoming increasingly rare. It's the ability to stay focused on long-term goals and values, rather than being swayed by the need for immediate rewards or validation. It requires strength of character to persist in the face of challenges, without seeking approval or acknowledgment from others.

The Code of the West embodies this principle by living with courage and acting with honor, even when the rewards aren't immediate.

Quiet diligence is about trusting that doing the right thing will pay off in the long run, even if it doesn't seem like it in the moment.

True leaders understand that their actions build a legacy, not just for themselves but for the people around them.

BEING INFORMED, NOT INFLAMED

In today's world, the lines between information and emotion are often blurred. Social media and news outlets are filled with content designed to provoke immediate reactions, whether it's anger, outrage, or joy. In this environment, it's easy to get swept up in the tide of emotion and forget to critically evaluate the information we're consuming. But true leadership requires a different approach: being informed, not inflamed.

Being informed means seeking out facts, perspectives, and knowledge from a variety of sources. It's about resisting the urge to react impulsively to headlines or posts and instead taking the time to understand the bigger picture. Leaders don't let themselves be swayed by the loudest voices. Rather, they look beyond the surface and question what's presented to them. In a world where misinformation and emotional manipulation are rampant, being informed is an act of quiet strength.

On the other hand, being inflamed is the opposite. It's allowing yourself to be driven by emotion, often without understanding the full context. It's easy to fall into echo chambers where our own beliefs are constantly reinforced, making it harder to see beyond our own perspective. When we're inflamed, we react based on impulse rather than reason, and in doing so, we lose the ability to lead with clarity and purpose.

Being informed, not inflamed, is about practicing discernment. It's about knowing when to step back from the noise, take a breath, and seek out the facts before forming an opinion. Leaders understand that knee-jerk reactions rarely lead to good decisions. Instead, they approach situations with a calm, measured mindset, knowing that true understanding takes time and effort.

In a world of emotional triggers and constant outrage, the ability to remain informed, thoughtful, and grounded is what sets true leaders apart. It's not about avoiding emotion but about not letting emotion drive every decision. The Code of the West teaches us to act with integrity and honor, and part of that is making decisions based on truth rather than feelings.

RESISTING POPULAR OPINION

In a world driven by trends, popularity, and the constant pressure to conform, resisting popular opinion is a rare form of leadership. It's easy to get swept up in the tide of what's current, especially when social media magnifies the voices of the majority. But true leaders don't follow the crowd for the sake of fitting in. They hold fast to their values, even when it means standing apart.

Resisting popular opinion doesn't mean rejecting everything mainstream. It's about having the discernment to know when a trend or belief doesn't align with your principles. This kind of leadership requires strength, not just to say no but to stand firm in your beliefs when everyone around you is pulling in a different direction. In a society that often equates agreement with unity, it takes real courage to stand alone.

This requires maintaining a healthy level of skepticism. Not everything popular is right, and not every majority opinion reflects reality. Morality and cultural beliefs can shift over time, but some truths transcend what's trendy or convenient and remain constant. It's like if a mob told you the sky was green, but you could see with your own eyes that the sky was blue. No matter how loud the crowd gets, the truth of what you see doesn't change. Leaders have to trust in what's real, even when others try to convince them otherwise.

At the heart of this is integrity. Leadership isn't about doing what's easiest or most popular but about doing what's right. And often what's right isn't what's popular. Leaders must be willing to question the status quo, to push back against the pressure to conform, and to stay true to themselves, even if it means going against the grain.

This doesn't mean rejecting collaboration or dialogue. It's about maintaining a clear sense of self in the midst of competing voices. Resisting popular opinion is about being open to listening to others but not being swayed by every new wave that comes along. True leadership is about setting your own course and following it with integrity, no matter where the crowd is headed.

The Code of the West embodies this principle. It teaches us to act with honor and courage, which sometimes means walking a lonely road. Leadership isn't about finding the easiest path. It's about finding the right one, even when it's the least traveled.

OWNING YOUR DECISIONS

Leadership isn't just about making choices. It's about taking responsibility for those choices, both in moments of success and when things go wrong. To own your decisions means to stand by the outcomes, whether they align with your expectations or not. It's the hallmark of true leadership: acknowledging that every choice you make carries weight and impact, not just for yourself but for others around you.

Owning your decisions requires self-awareness and accountability. Leaders don't pass the blame when things don't go as planned. Instead, they reflect on what could have been done differently and how to improve in the future. This mindset fosters growth, as every decision becomes an opportunity to learn, adapt, and grow stronger.

In today's world, it's easy to shift responsibility and blame circumstances, external forces, or other people for our missteps. But true leaders resist the urge to deflect. They understand that growth and integrity come from owning the full spectrum of their choices, the good and the bad. When a decision leads to success, a leader acknowledges the effort that went into it. When a decision doesn't go as planned, a leader faces it head-on and learns from it.

Owning your decisions doesn't mean being inflexible.

Leaders also recognize when it's time to adjust course or change their minds.

Flexibility and resilience are key traits of effective decision-making. The point isn't to stubbornly hold on to a bad decision but to have the humility to course-correct when necessary. It's about balancing conviction with the wisdom to evolve when needed.

At its core, owning your decisions is about living with integrity. It's about taking full responsibility for your actions, knowing that each choice reflects your values and shapes your legacy. The Code of the West teaches us to live with courage and act with honor, and part of that means standing by the decisions we make, no matter the outcome.

THE INFLUENCE OF EXAMPLE

Leadership isn't always about what you say; it's often more about what you *do.* People watch how you carry yourself, even when you don't realize it. Leading by example is one of the most powerful forms of leadership because it's authentic. It shows others not just what you believe but how you live those beliefs. Actions, more than words, inspire those around you.

What's key to remember is that this kind of leadership isn't dependent on age or status. Whether you're young or old, your actions can set an example. You don't need to wait until you've reached a level of experience to lead by example. A young person who lives with integrity, responsibility, and courage can have just as much impact as someone older. It's about embodying your values in everything you do, regardless of your age or position in life.

When you lead by example, you're not asking others to do something you wouldn't do yourself. You're showing what it looks like to live with integrity, courage, and purpose. Even if you don't think of yourself as a leader, your actions can have a profound influence on others. You may not always see it, but how you live sets a standard for the people around you, whether in your personal life, your community, or your workplace.

The influence of example is quiet but powerful. It's not about telling people how to live or what to believe; it's about showing them what living with honor and integrity looks like. It's the way you handle challenges, how you treat others, and the consistency with which you live out your values. This kind of leadership doesn't demand attention or recognition, but it leaves a lasting impact.

One of the key principles of the Code of the West is to live with courage and act with honor. When you lead by example, you embody these values in a way that words alone can't. Whether you realize it or not, your actions are shaping the world around you.

You're influencing the people who look up to you, those who rely on you, and even those who simply cross your path.

RESILIENCE AND ADAPTABILITY

Adaptability is often seen as the ability to roll with the punches and change course when circumstances shift. But true adaptability goes deeper than just responding to external forces. It's also about having the self-awareness and humility to recognize when you're wrong. In many ways, the most resilient leaders are those who aren't afraid to admit their mistakes, own their decisions, and make the necessary adjustments.

Part of adaptability is knowing when to let go of a course of action that isn't working. It's about being flexible, not just in how you respond to change but also in how you handle your own missteps. This ties back to owning your decisions and being willing to say, "I made the wrong call," and learning from it. Admitting you're wrong doesn't make you weak. In fact, it shows strength of character and the ability to grow from the experience.

Resilient leaders don't cling to the need to be right; they prioritize being effective. Sometimes that means acknowledging when new information comes to light and adapting based on that understanding. This doesn't apply just to external challenges but also to internal growth. The best leaders remain adaptable in their thinking, willing to change their minds when it's clear that a previous decision was flawed.

In the fast-paced, ever-changing modern world, resilience requires a mindset of growth. Instead of seeing mistakes as failures, resilient leaders see them as opportunities to learn. The ability to adapt isn't about avoiding mistakes but about how you handle them. Do you double down on a wrong decision, or do you have the humility to pivot, even when it's uncomfortable?

The Code of the West teaches us to live with integrity and act with honor. This includes being adaptable not just to the world around us but to our own growth. By acknowledging our mistakes and learning from them, we build resilience and become stronger leaders. True adaptability isn't about being perfect. It's about continuously evolving.

FINAL WORDS
Leadership by Choice

Leadership isn't something that's given to you. It's not a title you wait for or a reward that comes with time. Leadership is a choice. It's about stepping up when the moment calls for it, taking control of your own path, and living with integrity in everything you do. There's no ceremony or external validation—you're the one who has to make the decision to lead.

Leadership by choice means owning your actions, your decisions, and your mistakes. It's about leading by example, not waiting for someone to tell you it's your turn. True leadership is rooted in humility, in the ability to learn and adapt, and in the courage to stand by your values, even when the world pulls you in another direction.

In this section on leadership, we've explored the qualities that define modern leadership—quiet diligence, resilience, adaptability, and the willingness to resist popular opinion when it conflicts with what's right. But ultimately, all of these traits come down to one simple truth: Leadership is something you choose. It's something you take hold of for yourself, not because others ask you to but because you know it's the right thing to do.

The West wasn't built on dramatic heroics but on steady

application, day after day, showing up with integrity. The Code lives in the space between intention and action, where courage becomes the habit of facing what must be faced and honor becomes the practice of doing what's right regardless of audience. Leadership, at its core, is this intentional integration of principle into the common fabric of daily life.

Modern Living

SELF-SUFFICIENCY IN MODERN SOCIETY

In a world of instant conveniences, the idea of self-sufficiency might feel outdated, but it's more relevant than ever. True independence isn't about rejecting modern conveniences, but neither is it about being entirely reliant on them. Being self-sufficient means cultivating the skills and mindset to take care of yourself, make informed decisions, and solve problems without always needing external support.

At its core, self-sufficiency is about taking responsibility for your own life. It's not about isolating yourself or rejecting community but about being capable of thriving whether you have help or not.

PRACTICAL STEPS FOR BUILDING SELF-SUFFICIENCY

Develop Essential Skills: Learn life skills that make you more independent, like cooking from scratch, managing personal finances, or doing basic home repairs. These skills provide a sense of control over your environment so you're not constantly dependent on outside help.

Take Ownership of Your Health: Practice self-care and stay informed about your physical and mental health. Regular exercise, balanced nutrition, and mindfulness are key components of self-sufficiency. Knowing how to manage stress and maintain well-being builds a foundation for resilience.

Critical Thinking and Problem-Solving: Instead of accepting information at face value, practice critical thinking. In an age of information overload, it's vital to sift through sources and perspectives to make informed decisions. This strengthens your independence by reducing reliance on others for direction.

Embrace Resourcefulness: Cultivate resourcefulness by learning to make do with what you have. This doesn't mean rejecting modern technology but rather understanding how to manage your resources effectively. Whether it's growing your own food, repairing something instead of replacing it, or budgeting wisely, resourcefulness helps you stay resilient in any situation.

The Code of the West teaches self-reliance not as an act of isolation but as a way of living with purpose and responsibility. When you take ownership of your own life, you build the confidence and resilience needed to face modern challenges. Self-sufficiency is about empowering yourself to live fully, regardless of external circumstances.

RESILIENCE IN AN UNCERTAIN WORLD

The modern world is unpredictable. From personal challenges to global crises, uncertainty is a constant. Resilience is the ability to bounce back from setbacks and adapt in the face of adversity, and it is a skill that's more crucial than ever. But resilience isn't just about surviving; it's about thriving in the face of uncertainty, and it's a skill that can be cultivated.

Resilience doesn't come from avoiding difficulties. In fact, it's often the result of facing challenges head-on and learning to navigate them. Developing resilience is about building internal strength—mental, emotional, physical—so that when life throws you off course, you have the tools to recover and keep moving forward.

PRACTICAL STEPS FOR BUILDING RESILIENCE

Embrace Discomfort: Growth comes from discomfort. Intentionally put yourself in challenging situations, whether that's through physical challenges (like exercise or cold exposure) or mental challenges (like tackling something difficult at work). This can also include trying new activities you've always wanted to, like hiking or running a marathon. Remember it's about taking things one step at a time and acknowledging where you are at the start of the journey. You don't need to know everything at the beginning—just start.

Reframe Setbacks as Learning Opportunities: Every failure or setback holds a lesson. Instead of seeing difficulties as roadblocks, see them as stepping stones to improvement. After facing a challenge, reflect on what you learned and how you can apply it in the future.

Develop Emotional Regulation Skills: Resilience isn't just about external challenges. It's also about how you handle internal emotions. Practice techniques like mindfulness, deep breathing, or journaling to manage stress and remain calm under pressure. Emotional regulation is key to bouncing back quickly.

Maintain a Routine in Chaos: When the world feels unpredictable, having a consistent routine gives you a sense of control. It can start with something as simple as making your bed in the morning. Whether it's a morning ritual, a regular workout, or set times for deep work, routines help anchor you in stability even when external events are chaotic.

Cultivate a Growth Mindset: Embrace the idea that you can grow and improve through effort and learning. People with a growth mindset view challenges as

opportunities to develop new skills and strengths rather than threats to their competence. This mindset makes resilience a natural outcome of difficult situations.

The Code of the West teaches us to face challenges with courage and determination. Resilience isn't about never falling; it's about getting back up, time and time again. In an uncertain world, resilience gives you the strength to thrive, no matter what comes your way.

DIGITAL MINIMALISM AND MINDFULNESS

In an age of endless notifications and constant online engagement, the ability to focus has become a scarce commodity. Digital minimalism isn't about rejecting technology altogether; it's about using it with intention. The goal is to strip away the distractions that pull your attention away from what truly matters so you can create more space for focus, clarity, and meaningful connections.

Each ding or chime from your phone triggers a mental response that pulls you away from the present moment. This response isn't accidental; in reality, it's a result of classical conditioning, a psychological process where your brain associates certain cues (like a notification sound) with an immediate reward. Over time, we've been conditioned to expect a dopamine hit every time our phone buzzes.

It's the same mechanism that can keep us glued to our screens for hours, scrolling through endless feeds in search of the next reward.

But we don't have to be controlled by these triggers. By practicing digital minimalism and mindfulness, you can reclaim your attention and use technology in a way that serves your life.

PRACTICAL STEPS FOR DIGITAL MINIMALISM

Set Boundaries for Device Use: Designate specific times of day to be phone-free. Whether it's during meals, first thing in the morning, or the last hour before bed, these boundaries will help you disconnect and refocus.

Limit Social Media Check-Ins: Instead of mindlessly scrolling, set intentional windows of time to check social media or emails.

Utilize features like Instagram's quiet mode, which silences notifications for up to twelve hours, to create a more peaceful and less reactive environment. This prevents your phone from constantly chiming, which can create anxiety and allows you to check in at a time that works for you.

Understand the Triggers: Recognizing the power of classical conditioning can help you break free from the automatic pull of notifications. When you understand that your brain is seeking a reward, you can consciously choose not to engage with every buzz and beep.

Practice Single-Tasking: In a world that pushes for constant multitasking, practice focusing on one task at a time. This increases your productivity and reduces the mental exhaustion that comes from jumping between apps, tasks, and notifications.

Foster Real-Life Connections: Make an effort to prioritize in-person interactions over digital ones when possible. The depth of real-life conversations and experiences often outweighs the quick dopamine hits of online exchanges.

The Code of the West teaches us to live with integrity and purpose. In today's digital world, this means being mindful of where we place our attention and how we engage with technology. By practicing digital minimalism, we can regain control of our time and focus, allowing us to live more fully and with greater intention.

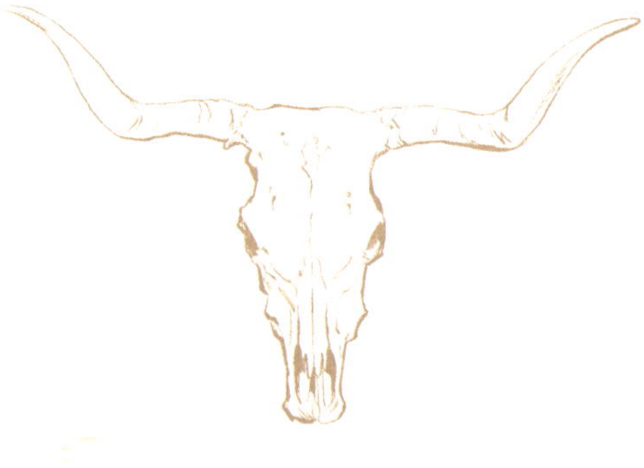

PURPOSE AND MEANING IN AN AGE OF DISTRACTION

In a world built up on the distractions of social media, endless entertainment, and constant notifications, it's easy to lose sight of what truly matters. We're surrounded by noise, and the signal that helps us find meaning and purpose can often get drowned out. But living with purpose means being intentional about what you give your attention to and grounding yourself in something bigger than the distractions around you.

When you know your "why," it becomes easier to resist the pull of distraction and focus on the things that truly matter. Purpose gives you direction, even in chaotic times.

One of the most important skills in finding meaning is learning to say no. In a world that's connected 24-7, we are constantly being pulled in different directions. Whether it's a social invitation, a phone call, or a text message, there's often a feeling of obligation to always be available or to say yes to everything that comes our way.

But real purpose comes from making your time a priority and recognizing that you are not obligated to constantly be at the mercy of your phone or other people's demands. Setting boundaries around your time is crucial for mental health and for ensuring that you stay aligned with your goals and values.

PRACTICAL STEPS FOR FINDING PURPOSE AND MEANING

Clarify Your Values: Take time to reflect on what matters most to you. What are the core principles that guide your decisions? Once you know what's truly important, you can align your daily actions with those values.

Learn to Say No: Saying no is a powerful tool in protecting your time and energy. You are not obligated to always be available or to say yes to every invitation or request. By setting boundaries and making your time a priority, you free up space for the things that matter most.

Limit Distractions with Intention: Distractions are inevitable, but how you manage them is within your control. By setting clear boundaries, you create space for deeper engagement with the things that bring you fulfillment.

Practice Mindful Goal-Setting: Purpose doesn't need to be a lofty ideal. Rather, it should be something you can work toward every day. Set goals that are aligned with your values, and break them down into manageable steps. Every small action that moves you toward your goals reinforces a sense of purpose.

Create Time for Reflection: In the hustle of modern life, it's easy to go through the motions without ever stopping to reflect. Set aside time regularly to evaluate where you are and whether your actions are aligned with your values and long-term goals.

Seek Out Activities That Enrich You: Whether it's a creative project, volunteering, or spending time with loved ones, invest time in activities that nourish your sense of meaning. These activities remind you of what's truly important, even when distractions are pulling at you.

The Code of the West teaches us to live with courage, integrity, and purpose. In a world full of distractions, the ability to find meaning in your actions and decisions is more important than ever. By grounding yourself in your values and taking intentional steps toward your goals, you can navigate the chaos with clarity and purpose.

AUTHENTICITY IN A PERFORMATIVE WORLD

In today's world, it's easy to fall into the trap of performing. Social media, workplace expectations, and even social circles can create pressure to present a curated version of ourselves that fits into what we think others want to see. This constant performance can be exhausting, and over time, it can distance us from who we truly are. Authenticity, on the other hand, is about living in alignment with our true selves, not just when it's easy but especially when it's challenging.

Being authentic means embracing who you are without needing to seek external validation. It's about showing up as yourself, flaws and all, and resisting the urge to change in order to meet the expectations of others. In a performative world, where likes, comments, and approval can feel like currency, authenticity is a radical act of self-respect and courage.

PRACTICAL STEPS FOR CULTIVATING AUTHENTICITY

Know Your Values: The foundation of authenticity is clarity about your own values. Spend time understanding what drives you, what you believe in, and what matters most to you. When you're grounded in your values, it's easier to stay true to yourself in any situation.

Embrace Imperfections: No one is perfect, and authenticity means owning your imperfections instead of hiding them. By showing up as your full self, you encourage others to do the same. It's not about being flawless; it's about being real.

Resist External Validation: In a world that rewards performance, it's easy to seek approval from others. But true fulfillment comes from living according to your own standards, not the praise of others. Challenge yourself to detach from the need for likes, compliments, or validation from external sources.

Set Boundaries with Social Media: Social media often encourages performance over authenticity. Be mindful of how much time you spend curating an online persona versus living authentically offline. Set limits for how you engage with social platforms, and prioritize real-life connections and experiences over digital approval.

Speak Your Truth: Authenticity is also about having the courage to speak your mind, even when it's uncomfortable. This doesn't mean being abrasive or inconsiderate but rather standing firm in what you believe and sharing your thoughts with honesty and respect.

The Code of the West teaches us to live with integrity, which is impossible without authenticity. In a world that often encourages performance, living authentically means staying grounded in who you are and what you believe in, no matter the pressure to conform. It's not about playing a role; it's about being true to yourself and letting that truth guide your actions.

BALANCING INDIVIDUALITY AND COMMUNITY

One of the greatest tensions in modern life is finding the balance between being true to yourself and contributing meaningfully to a community. In the pursuit of individuality, it's easy to feel disconnected, but in fully giving yourself to a group or cause, you can sometimes lose sight of your own identity. The challenge is to find a way to honor your own values and autonomy while also recognizing that we are all part of something bigger.

Being part of a community doesn't mean sacrificing your individuality. In fact, the healthiest communities are built on individuals who bring their unique strengths, perspectives, and values into the collective. The balance lies in knowing when to stand firm in who you are and when to lean into the needs of the group, recognizing that both are necessary for a fulfilling life.

It's also important to protect yourself from group dynamics that may become toxic or enabling. Sometimes, being part of a group can blind you to behaviors or patterns that aren't healthy for you. In these moments, it's crucial to know when it's time to step away for your own well-being. The right community will support you in being your best self, but it's up to you to recognize when you need to protect yourself from negative influences.

PRACTICAL STEPS FOR BALANCING INDIVIDUALITY AND COMMUNITY

Know When to Stand Your Ground: It's important to be able to say no when something goes against your values. Being part of a community doesn't mean you need to agree with everything or go along with the crowd. Authenticity and individuality are about standing firm when it matters most.

Contribute Your Strengths: Every individual has unique talents and abilities. Bringing your own strengths to the table helps strengthen the community as a whole. Look for ways you can offer your skills and perspective to enrich the group without losing sight of who you are.

Practice Active Listening: Part of being a valuable community member is being open to the perspectives and needs of others. Practice listening actively, even when you don't agree, and seek to understand before seeking to be understood. This fosters mutual respect while maintaining your own point of view.

Set Healthy Boundaries: Sometimes, in an effort to be helpful or involved, we can overextend ourselves, sacrificing our own needs in the process. Learn to set boundaries that protect your time and energy, allowing you to contribute to the community without feeling drained or overwhelmed.

Foster Meaningful Connections: Individuality doesn't mean isolation. Seek out meaningful connections within your community that allow you to stay true to yourself while also contributing to the greater good. These relationships should enrich both you and the collective.

The Code of the West teaches us the importance of both riding for the brand and staying true to who we are. It's not an either-or proposition—it's about knowing when to lean into the needs of the community and when to stand firm in your individuality. By balancing both, you become a stronger individual and a more valuable member of the collective.

SELF-SUFFICIENCY IN MODERN SOCIETY

In the modern world, the idea of self-sufficiency can sometimes feel like a relic of the past. With everything at our fingertips, from groceries delivered to our door to the answers to any question available in seconds, it's easy to become dependent on convenience. But true self-sufficiency isn't about rejecting modern conveniences; it's about cultivating the skills and mindset to rely on yourself when necessary.

Self-sufficiency means being able to handle life's challenges without always needing outside help. It's about building the confidence and capability to solve problems, whether practical or emotional. In a world that often prioritizes quick fixes and easy solutions, self-sufficiency offers a sense of freedom and empowerment that comes from knowing you can take care of yourself.

PRACTICAL STEPS FOR BUILDING SELF-SUFFICIENCY

Develop Basic Life Skills: From cooking your own meals to managing your finances, self-sufficiency starts with mastering basic life skills. These small, everyday actions build the foundation of self-reliance and ensure that you can meet your own needs.

Learn Problem-Solving Skills: When you encounter a problem, instead of immediately turning to others for solutions, challenge yourself to figure it out. Whether it's fixing something around the house or working through a personal issue, practice developing your own solutions.

Build Resilience through Discomfort: Self-sufficiency requires resilience. Putting yourself in uncomfortable situations—whether through physical challenges, like learning a new skill, or emotional ones, like facing a difficult conversation—helps you build the strength to handle life's uncertainties.

Embrace a DIY Mindset: Whenever possible, look for opportunities to do things yourself rather than outsourcing. This could mean growing your own vegetables, repairing something around the house, or learning how to budget and manage your finances. These practices build confidence and capability.

Foster Resourcefulness: Part of self-sufficiency is learning to use what you have at hand. Instead of immediately buying new things or seeking external help, challenge yourself to make do with what's available. Resourcefulness helps you adapt and thrive in any situation.

The Code of the West teaches us the importance of self-reliance and personal responsibility. In a world that often encourages dependence on external systems, cultivating self-sufficiency helps you take ownership of your life. It empowers you to meet challenges head-on, knowing you have the skills and resilience to succeed on your own terms.

DISCOMFORT AS A PATH TO GROWTH

In a society that prioritizes comfort and convenience, the idea of seeking discomfort can seem counterintuitive. Yet discomfort is one of the most powerful drivers of personal growth. True growth, whether physical, mental, or emotional, rarely happens when we stay in our comfort zone.

Discomfort doesn't have to mean extreme hardship. It can be as simple as trying something new, tackling a difficult project, or pushing yourself just a little harder in your daily routine. When we embrace discomfort, we stretch our limits, build resilience, and open ourselves up to new possibilities.

PRACTICAL STEPS FOR EMBRACING DISCOMFORT

Start Small: Growth doesn't happen overnight, and it doesn't require huge leaps. Start with small discomforts. Whether it's trying a new activity, like hiking, or challenging yourself to have a difficult conversation, the key is to begin stepping outside your comfort zone, little by little.

Acknowledge Where You Are: Growth requires honesty. Acknowledge your starting point, and give yourself grace for not being perfect right away. Whether you're learning a new skill or embarking on a physical challenge, accept that you'll likely stumble at the start. The important part is to keep going.

Push Your Physical Limits: Physical discomfort, whether through exercise or challenging outdoor activities, can be a gateway to mental resilience. By pushing your body, you strengthen your mind, learning to cope with discomfort in other areas of life.

Reframe Failure as Learning: Discomfort often comes with failure, but each failure is an opportunity to learn. Instead of fearing mistakes, see them as stepping stones toward improvement. Growth comes from the lessons learned in moments of discomfort, not from avoiding those moments altogether.

Embrace Uncertainty: Life is full of unknowns, and trying to control every outcome can create unnecessary stress. Instead, embrace uncertainty as part of the journey. Discomfort in uncertain situations helps you adapt and strengthens your ability to handle whatever life throws your way.

One of the key components to continued personal development is embracing the mindset of a lifelong student.

By continuously challenging yourself, you tap into the brain's neuroplasticity, which is its ability to adapt and reorganize itself through new experiences and learning. If you don't push your limits and seek out new challenges, you risk becoming rigid in both your thinking and your existence. Stagnation sets in when you stop learning, and remaining flexible and open to growth is essential for staying resilient and thriving in an ever-changing world.

By embracing discomfort, we open ourselves up to growth, resilience, and the strength to thrive in an unpredictable world.

FINAL WORDS
A Guide to Self-Directed Learning

This section, and indeed this entire manual, has been designed as a guide, *not a prescription.* It's meant to inspire self-directed learning, encouraging you to take the principles of the Code of the West and apply them in your own life in ways that make sense for you. The topics we've covered, such as modern leadership, social media, individuality, resilience, discomfort, and more, are broad concepts, each with their own depths to explore. But what matters most is how you integrate these lessons into your own path.

This isn't the final word on the Code of the West. Rather, it's the beginning of a journey. In future works, we may dive deeper into these ideas, exploring them in more granular, nuanced ways. But the goal of this manual is to provide you with the foundation to begin charting your own course.

The world around us is constantly changing, and the challenges we face, whether personal, social, or cultural, are always evolving.

But the principles within the Code of the West are timeless. They provide a compass that can guide you through uncertainty, help you stay grounded in your values, and empower you to live with purpose and integrity.

As you continue forward, remember that this manual is just a starting point. The real work lies in applying these ideas to your own life and continuing to grow, learn, and challenge yourself along the way.

It's not about following a strict set of rules; it's about staying true to the core principles of courage, honor, and self-reliance. In doing so, you become part of the greater mission to bring back America's shared story and to live a life of meaning in an ever-changing world.

This is the final section in the Code of the West manual. Now it's time to take what you've learned and apply it to the real world. The journey is yours to create.

EPILOGUE
A Call to Action

At the heart of Code of the West is a mission: to bring back America's shared story. In a time when it often feels like we're more divided than united, this mission is about finding the common ground that has always been a part of our collective identity. It's about reclaiming the values that make us who we are and writing a new chapter in that shared story.

This manual is intended to be more than just a guide; it's a call to prepare you to play your part in that mission. Every principle, every lesson, and every piece of advice was meant to equip you with the tools to live with purpose, to lead, and to take action in your own life. The ideas in this book aren't just meant for the page, *they're meant for the field.* You are part of this story, and what you do next matters.

If you found value in these pages, and if you believe in the mission of Code of the West, I ask that you help spread the word. Share this book with someone who needs it. Pass it along to a friend, a family member, or a colleague. Give it to someone who is searching for meaning, purpose, or guidance. The more we share this message, the more we can help bring back that shared story we all crave.

If you're inspired, leave a review, especially on Amazon. Reviews are how others find their way to books like this one. The more reviews we garner, the greater the chance that someone else who needs this message will come across it.

Yes, leaving a review helps sell more books, but that's not the goal here. It's about allowing people to organically find this manual, just as you did, so they can join the mission, too.

Tag us on social media. Whether it's on Instagram, Facebook, or Twitter/X, use the hashtag #LiveTheCode to show how you're putting these principles into practice. Share your journey and inspire others to live the Code in their own way.

But most importantly, go and LIVE.

This isn't just a book—it's a way of life. It's about embodying the principles of honor, integrity, and purpose every single day.

Ride for the brand. Make the commitment, not just to yourself but to something bigger. Because when you live the Code, you become part of the mission to bring back America's shared story.

ACKNOWLEDGMENTS

For as long as I can remember, I've been looking toward a western horizon. Despite being born in Ohio, my earliest memories are of the Pacific Ocean, the Mojave Desert, and the sun setting over both of them.

My dad was a truck driver. My memories of the road begin in the late 1980s in a world of CB radios tuned to channel 19 and Sawyer Brown cassettes playing in the cab. I remember the chicken lights zipping past in the eastbound lanes while my dad and I chased the setting sun, hanging over the extended hood of a Kenworth W900. In that cab, across thousands of miles, I learned the power of silence. I learned that, sometimes, just being there is enough.

I was a sick kid. Asthma, allergies, and seizures compounded in a way that left me effectively deaf just as I was supposed to be learning to speak. When I should have been learning to read, I was still catching up on how to make sounds that people could understand. I spent the first few years of my life just waiting for the intermittent moments when I wasn't sick or suffering.

Throughout all of it, my mom was my defender. Despite my disabilities, she pushed me toward autonomy so I could participate in my own survival. By the time she asked if I wanted to move to Idaho at age nine, I'd already knocked on death's door and learned to speak at a school for the deaf.

Because of her, I learned that when you think you've hit the limit, you're usually just getting started. In 1994, my mom and I packed a tiny car and cannonballed from Columbus, Ohio, to Boise, Idaho. From that point on, the West became my home. The West didn't make me; it just gave me the room to build myself. The job of making me belonged to my stepdad. He was a cowboy from northern California who took me on as a project when he married my mom. Plenty of people told me I could do anything I wanted. He showed me how to actually pick up the tools and do it.

And so here we are. I'm writing the acknowledgment for a book that I shouldn't be able to read, let alone write.

To the mentors who held the light and the friends who became family, I thank you. And to the ones I've lost, I hope you know that you are still part of the push. You all made me the man I am today.

I'm grateful that I held on long enough to learn and grow from my mistakes, and I am grateful to have the opportunity to speak to you here in these pages, something that wouldn't have been possible without a kind and open-minded editor in Kate Zimmermann, who was willing to take a chance with a rough-around-the-edges stranger out west. To the team at Andrews McMeel, thank you for giving these words a home and for putting in the work to elevate this book above something I could have done alone.

The West is as wild as you want it to be. You don't need to have the answers before you arrive—it will teach you once you're here, so long as you're open to learning the lessons.

The key is to simply first go west.

ABOUT THE AUTHOR

Chris Hunt is a storyteller and creator with a diverse background that includes working as a comic book artist and as the former art director for Black Rifle Coffee, where his work helped elevate the brand. He is the founder of Code of the West, a platform that blends his passion for storytelling, philosophy, and Western values. When he's not writing or creating, Chris can be found documenting the real cowboys and cowgirls of the West, capturing their stories and way of life. He lives by the belief that a personal code is essential to navigating life with integrity and purpose.

Instagram: @TheCodeOfTheWest
YouTube: @the_codeofthewest
Substack: cotw.substack.com